# Rock

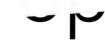

## London

rom bedsit to stadium,
laces where the
tars made it happen

the handbook guide

First published in 1997 by
Handbook Publishing Ltd, 14 Anhalt Road, London SW11 4NX



ISBN 1-901309-01-0

Printed in England by Biddles Ltd, Guildford and Kings Lynn

Compiled and edited by Crail Low and Lucy Minto
Book and cover design by Ivan Bulloch

Maps compiled from the 1939 John Bartholomew Atlas revised from copyright free aerial photography and checked on foot. Drawn and produced by Landfall Mapping, Southampton (01703) 7300099/585041

Cover photographs: The Beatles by Terence Spencer © Camera Press and Oasis © Retna Pictures Ltd

Photographs © Crail Low, except: pages 6-7, 30-31, 56-57, 60, 128-129 © Rex, 14-15, 22-23, 28, 38, 40-41, 44 (left), 46, 50-51, 64, 72, 148, 160, 166, 171, 172 © Pictorial Press, 68-69 © PA News, 168-169 © Christie's Images

**Other titles in the series**

Royal Life: Town & Country

**Forthcoming titles**

The River Thames

Villages of London

Gardens & Wildlife in London

Film & TV: Location London

Royal Britain

Rock & Pop Britain

# Contents

# LONDON: A Capital of Music

In 1953 Elizabeth II was crowned Queen at Westminster. The nation celebrated hoping stability had returned and the post-war gloom had passed. High society set the style and the establishment set the rules. Everybody knew their place and the young did what they were told.

### A Wop Bop Alul Bop A Wop Bam Boom

Then from America, rock 'n' roll came. Little Richard, Chuck Berry, Elvis Presley and Jerry Lee Lewis shouted that life could be different and you could be somebody without a dinner jacket or posh accent. Teenagers throughout England responded to the call.

Harry Webb, Terry Nelhams and Thomas Hicks were the first. They coiffed their hair, sharpened their sneers and got to Soho to become Cliff Richard, Adam Faith and Tommy Steel.

In 1963 the Beatles arrived from Liverpool and London became the centre of pop music.

From Dartford to Pinner, London's suburbs gave birth to the new stars. The Rolling Stones, The Who, The Kinks, Eric Clapton, Rod Stewart, Elton John: all called London home.

The streets pulsated with their energy. And their songs were the art form that defined the age: *Street Fighting Man, A Day In The Life* and *My Generation* mirrored the events, attitudes and emotions of youth.

### Picture Yourself In A Boat On A River
### With Tangerine Trees And Marmalade Skies

By 1970, pop stars were the new establishment - a society of the gifted, beautiful and young. But this was also under threat: Jimi Hendrix and Brian Jones were dead; The Beatles had split; The Stones were tax exiles; and Eric Clapton, Syd Barrett and many others, lost in drugs.

Luckily, a new wave came to the rescue. Marc Bolan from Wimbledon and David Bowie from Beckenham led the charts through Glam Rock, wearing lipstick and high heels, whilst from the London universities and grand public schools, Genesis, Pink Floyd and Queen gave pop music greater credibility.

### God save the Queen, she ain't no human being.
### She's made you a moron

Pop celebrated the Queen's Silver Jubilee in 1977 with a return to basics. From the tower blocks of London's decaying suburbs, spotty delinquents with names like Rotten and Vicious made their way to the King's Road to shops with names like Sex. There, dressed in fetish clothes, they screamed at the world. Though unable to play like the super groups, they had as much to say and with more attitude.

**I'm A Soul Boy - I'm A Dole Boy**
**Take Pleasure In Leisure, I Believe In Joy!**

Five years on and London's economy was in trouble. With industry closing down and unemployment exceeding three million, no-one wanted to feel more depressed. Music lost its rough edges as people wanted escape.

At clubs like Heroes, Camden Palace and Heaven, they danced through the night to Spandau Ballet, Boy George and Wham!. After all there was seldom a job to get up for the next day.

In 1984, Bob Geldof woke up in Clapham to news of the Ethiopian famine. So began a £100 million charity, the biggest selling single and the world's most watched pop concert at Wembley. Band Aid gave pop the acknowledgement it had always deserved. The stars now mixed with the country's elite: many were richer than royalty and had careers more stable than the civil service.

But back in the teenage bedroom, three chords and a back-beat continued through Oasis, Pulp, Suede and Blur...

**Today Is Gonna Be The Day**
**That They're Gonna Throw It Back To You**

## HOW TO USE THIS BOOK

This guidebook to Rock & Pop is based on geographical areas of London. It is not a biography of rock and pop, but rather sets out the areas and places where events happened that are significant to this important art form.

Each entry is listed with the address, what happened and when.

Each of the central areas has a map which shows the numbered entries. In addition there are maps for other important areas, such as The Rolling Stones' Dartford and The Beatles' Liverpool. There is also a locator map for Greater London.

At the end of the book, the index is compiled around the names of the personalities and groups.

**Notes on the text:**

**1** Song titles are written in italics, e.g. *Yesterday*, *Careless Whisper* etc
**2** Song lyrics are written in italics with quotation marks, e.g. *"I read the news today, oh boy, about a lucky man who made the grade"*.
**3** Titles of books, newspapers, television programmes and films etc. are with single quotation marks, e.g. 'Top of the Pops' and 'The Sunday Times'.
**4** Speech has double quotation marks.

Blur shooting a promotional video on the roof of **HMV** on Oxford Street

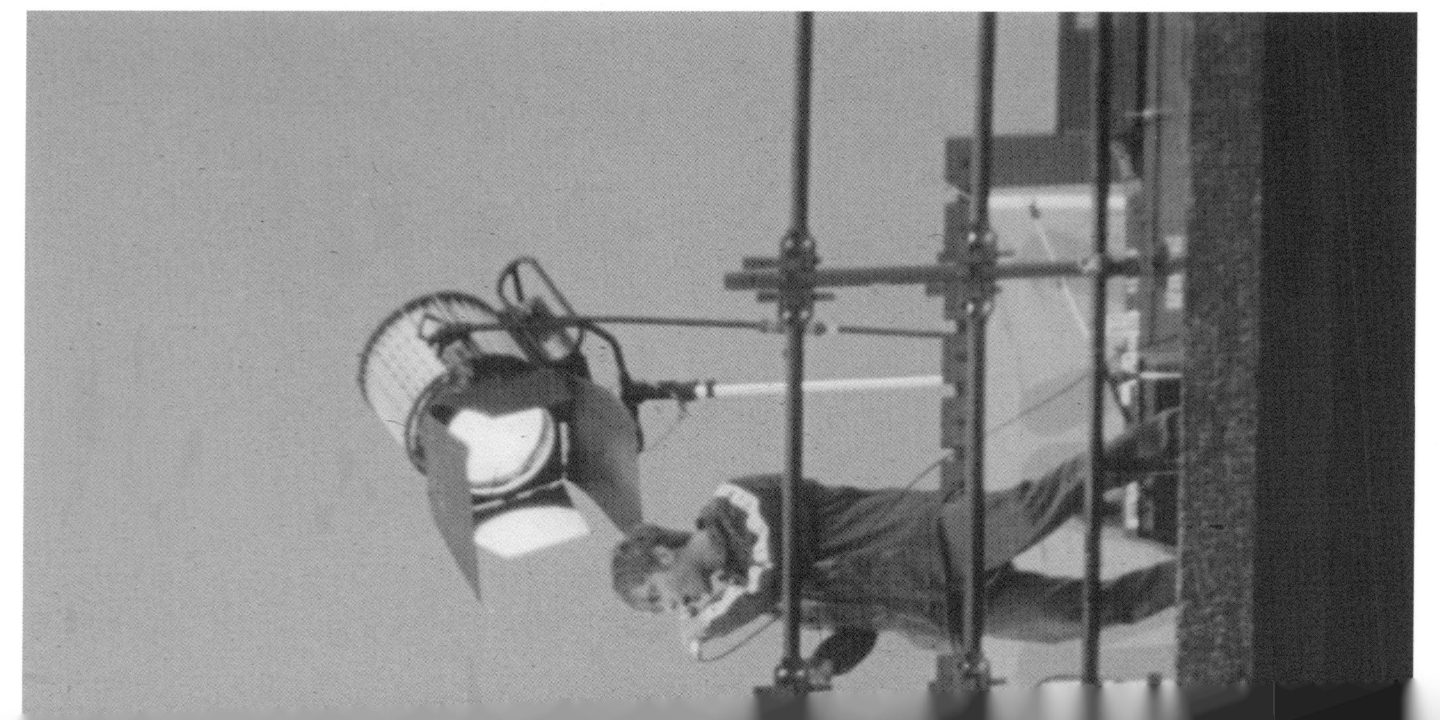

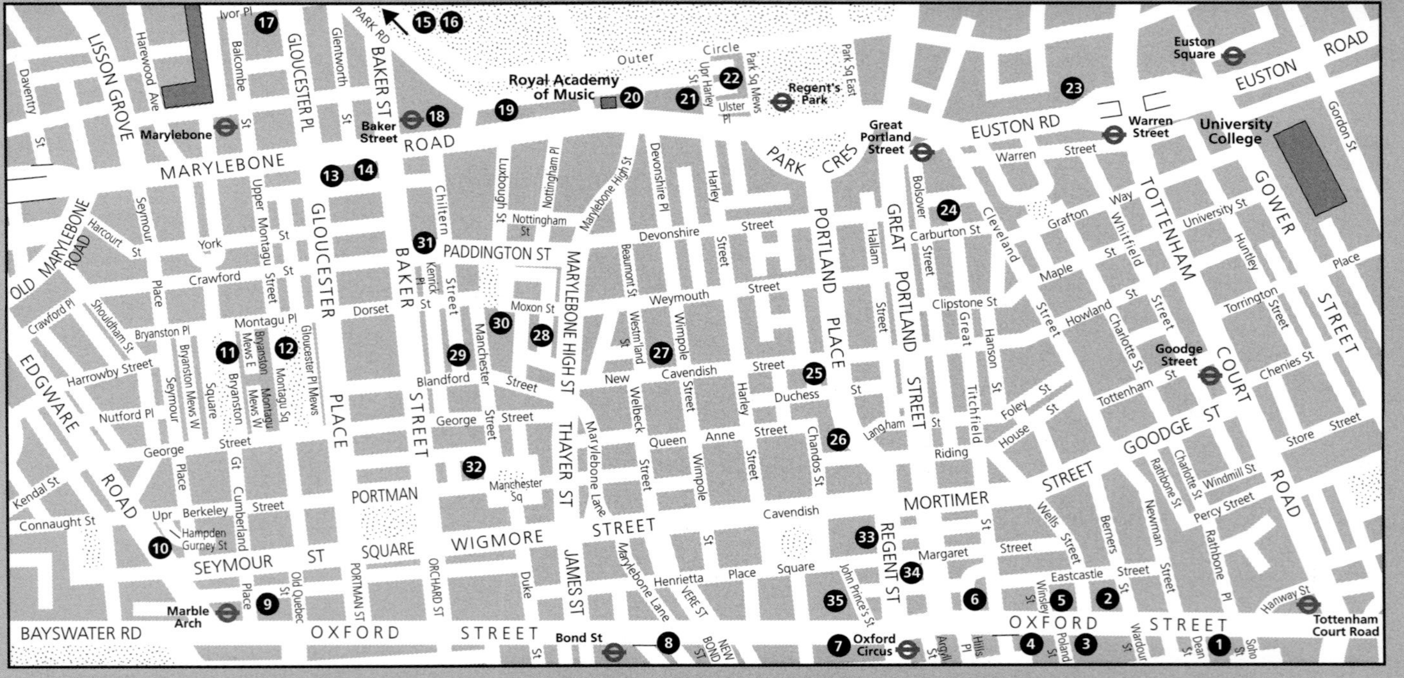


**Central London** Oxford Street W1|NW1

# Oxford Street W1|NW1



1 | Where: 79 Oxford Street, Beat City
Who: **THE SPENCER DAVIS GROUP**
When: 1965

Chris Blackwell, owner of Island Records, had recently signed this Birmingham group and organised their first London gig at this leading club.

Within months, their breakthrough record *Keep On Running* was released.

The group's 16 year old vocalist, Steve Winwood, left in 1967 to form Traffic, and briefly Blind Faith, before going on to a successful solo career.

2 | Where: 100 Oxford Street, 100 Club
Who: **THE SEX PISTOLS/SIOUXSIE & THE BANSHEES**
When: 20-21 September 1976

Site of the famous punk festival.

It was Siouxsie and The Banshees' first gig and Sid Vicious, friend of The Sex Pistols' Johnny Rotten, was playing drums.

During the festival, Sid lashed a bike chain at music journalist Nick Kent (who had taught Steve Jones of The Pistols how to play guitar). He also smashed a glass that blinded a member of the audience, before being arrested for carrying a knife.

The first punk 'festival' had been held at The Marquee Club in February 1976 and another at the Screen On The Green in Islington in August.

Sid Vicious auditioned for The Sex Pistols in February 1977 at the Blue Posts Pub on Tottenham Court Road. Although he only had basic musical skills, he was preferable to Glen Matlock who was fired, according to Johnny Rotten, for "liking The Beatles".

3 | Where: 119 Oxford Street, Dryden Chambers
Who: **THE SEX PISTOLS**
When: 1976

Malcolm McLaren, manager of The Sex Pistols, shared offices in this building, along with Miles Copeland, manager of The Police. McLaren's company was called Glitterbest Management.

His career began at Harrow Art College, where he met Vivienne Westwood, and later at Goldsmiths College, from 1968-1971. McLaren and Westwood then set up a shop to sell their extreme fashion clothes on the King's Road, Chelsea.

4 | Where: 165 Oxford Street, The Marquee Club
When: Early 1960s

**THE ROLLING STONES** played their first gig here on 12 July 1962. Consisting of Mick Jagger, Keith Richard, Brian Jones, Ian Chapman, Ian Stewart, Geoff Bradford and Dick Taylor, they stood in for Blues Incorporated who could not play that night.

A couple of months before, in March 1962, Brian Jones had seen Muddy Waters perform at The Marquee. This inspired him to form a rhythm and blues band and the following day he advertised for musicians under the alias of Elmo Lewis in 'Jazz News'. The band needed a name: *Rollin' Stone* was the title of a 1950 Muddy Waters' song.

Also...

**ROD STEWART** made his professional debut at the club with Long John Baldry and The Hoochie Coochie Men on 6 January 1964.

**5** | Where: Winsley Street, Mappin House
Who: **THE PET SHOP BOYS**
When: 1980s

Current offices of Smash Hits magazine. They moved here from 52-55 Carnaby Street, where Neil Tennant had been an assistant editor for the magazine. In the early 1980s he met Chris Lowe in a hi-fi shop on the King's Road, Chelsea. They were both already in bands, but, after meeting, began to write songs together. In 1984 the Pet Shop Boys released their first single, *West End Girls*.

**6** | Where: 214 Oxford Street, Air Studios
When: 1980s

Air Studios belong to George Martin, the ex-EMI and Beatles record producer. **PAUL McCARTNEY** recorded *Tug of War* here in May 1982 with contributions from Stevie Wonder, Carl Perkins and Ringo Starr. The album reached No.1 in the UK. The cover shot of McCartney was taken by Linda in the studio.

Also...

**THE JAM** recorded *A Town Called Malice* in the studios in 1982.

Also...

**THE PRETENDERS** were photographed on the rooftop of the studios at the end of 1983 for their album *Learning to Crawl*.

Also...

**ELTON JOHN** met Renate Blauel, a tape operator, at Air Studios when he was recording *Too Low for Zero* in early 1983. They married in Sydney, Australia on 14 February 1984 with Bernie Taupin, his song-writing partner, as best man. They divorced in November 1988.

**7** | Where: Oxford Street, Salvation Army HQ
Who: **ELTON JOHN**
When: 1967

Whilst recording his first album, Elton John was penniless and had to stay here. *Empty Skies* was released in June 1967 and contained the first collection of Elton John and Bernie Taupin songs. Elton recalled:

> "We used to walk back from the sessions at about four in the morning and stay at the Salvation Army headquarters in Oxford Street. Steve Brown's [the producer] dad used to run the place, and he used to live above it. I used to sleep on the sofa."

**8** | Where: 363 Oxford Street, HMV
When: 1950s & 1960s

**CLIFF RICHARD & THE SHADOWS**, then known as Harry Webb & The Drifters, recorded their first demo disc at HMV for £10 in early 1958. The two songs were *Lawdy Miss Clawdy* and *Breathless*. The demo was financed by the parents of manager, John Foster.

And...

**THE BEATLES'** career began here in early 1962, when the demo tape from their failed Decca audition was heard by George Martin in offices above HMV.

The tape had been recommended by an engineer at the Decca audition. Martin was impressed enough to sign them to EMI without a formal audition. He told The Beatles' manager Brian Epstein, "I know very little about groups, Brian, but I believe you have something very good here".

**9** | Where: Great Cumberland Place, Cumberland Hotel
Who: **JIMI HENDRIX**
When: 18 September 1970

Jimi Hendrix died in Rooms 507-508 of the Cumberland Hotel. His death was caused by a drug overdose that he had taken earlier in the evening at his girlfriend's flat in Notting Hill Gate. He had spent part of his last day shopping at Kensington Market on High Street Kensington.

**10** | Where: Hampden Gurney Street, Nemo Studios
Who: **JON & VANGELIS YES**
When: 1981-1982

The music for the film 'Chariots of Fire' was recorded at Nemo Studios, winning the composer, Vangelis Papathanassiou, an Oscar.

The studios belonged to Vangelis, who teamed up with Jon Anderson of Yes to record several albums here including *Short Stories* and *Waiting for Mr Cairo*.

**Bryanston Mews**

**11** | Where: 13a Bryanston Mews East
Who: **MICK JAGGER-THE ROLLING STONES**
When: Spring 1965-Early 1966

This small modern mews house was where Mick Jagger lived by himself for the first time. He moved here after a couple of years of sharing flats and houses with the rest of the band.

**12** | Where: 34 Montagu Square
Who: **THE BEATLES & JIMI HENDRIX**
When: 1965-1969

**RINGO STARR** bought this flat in 1965 and sold it on 28 February 1969 after problems caused by the friends he rented it out to.
First...
**JIMI HENDRIX** rented the flat with his manager Chas Chandler for three months, from December 1966 to March 1967. Starr evicted Hendrix and Chandler after they painted all the rooms black and used only candles for light. He sued Hendrix for damages and the case was settled out of court.
Then...
**JOHN LENNON** moved into the flat in July 1968, with Yoko Ono, after leaving Cynthia, his wife. Montagu Square was the first place that Lennon and Ono lived together as a couple and Lennon was happy to move back to London after his time in suburban Weybridge. The flat was also the scene of their drug bust by the police on 18 October 1968.

The cover photograph for their joint album, *Unfinished Music No.1 - Two Virgins*, was taken in the flat. The controversial cover featured the two lovers completely naked and was taken by Lennon on a delayed-timer camera. EMI did not wish to associate themselves with the album and so it was distributed by another company, Track, who sold the record wrapped in a paper bag.

After Lennon's activities caused complaints from many local residents, Ringo Starr sold the flat.

"When two great Saints meet it is a humbling experience. The long battles to prove he was a Saint."—Paul McCartney
Unfinished Music No. 1. Two Virgins. Yoko Ono/John Lennon

**34 Montagu Square**

**13** | Where: Gloucester Place, Marylebone Registry Office
Who: **THE BEATLES & OASIS**

Here, on 12 March 1969 Paul McCartney married Linda Eastman and on 26 April 1981 Ringo Starr married Barbara Bach. Liam Gallagher married Patsy Kensit here on 17 April 1997, at 8.30am, after they postponed their wedding in February.

**14** | Where: 181 Marylebone Road, Marylebone Magistrates Court
When: 1960s & 1970s

**JOHN LENNON** and **YOKO ONO** appeared before the court charged with possession of cannabis on 28 November 1968. Ono was pregnant at the time and soon after had a miscarriage. She was acquitted, but Lennon was found guilty and fined £150. The conviction was to cause problems for his application for residency in the United States in the 1970s.

Also...

**THE SEX PISTOLS'** Sid Vicious, and his girlfriend, Nancy Spungen, appeared before the Court on amphetamine charges on 12 May 1978. The trial was held at Knightsbridge Crown Court.

**15** | Where: 25 Hanover Gate Mansions, Park Road
Who: **JOHN LENNON & YOKO ONO**
When: January 1967-July 1968

Yoko Ono lived in this block of flats, opposite Kent Passage, with her husband Tony Cox until she moved into Montagu Square with John Lennon.

**16** | Where: Park Road, London Central Mosque
Who: **CAT STEVENS**
When: 1979

Cat Stevens converted to Islam and lived at the Mosque for a while. On his conversion, Stevens changed his name to Yusuf Islam and in September married Fouzie Ali at the Kensington Mosque. He gave up music in February 1979 to devote his time to the Islamic Schools Trust at 8 Brondesbury Park, West Hampstead.

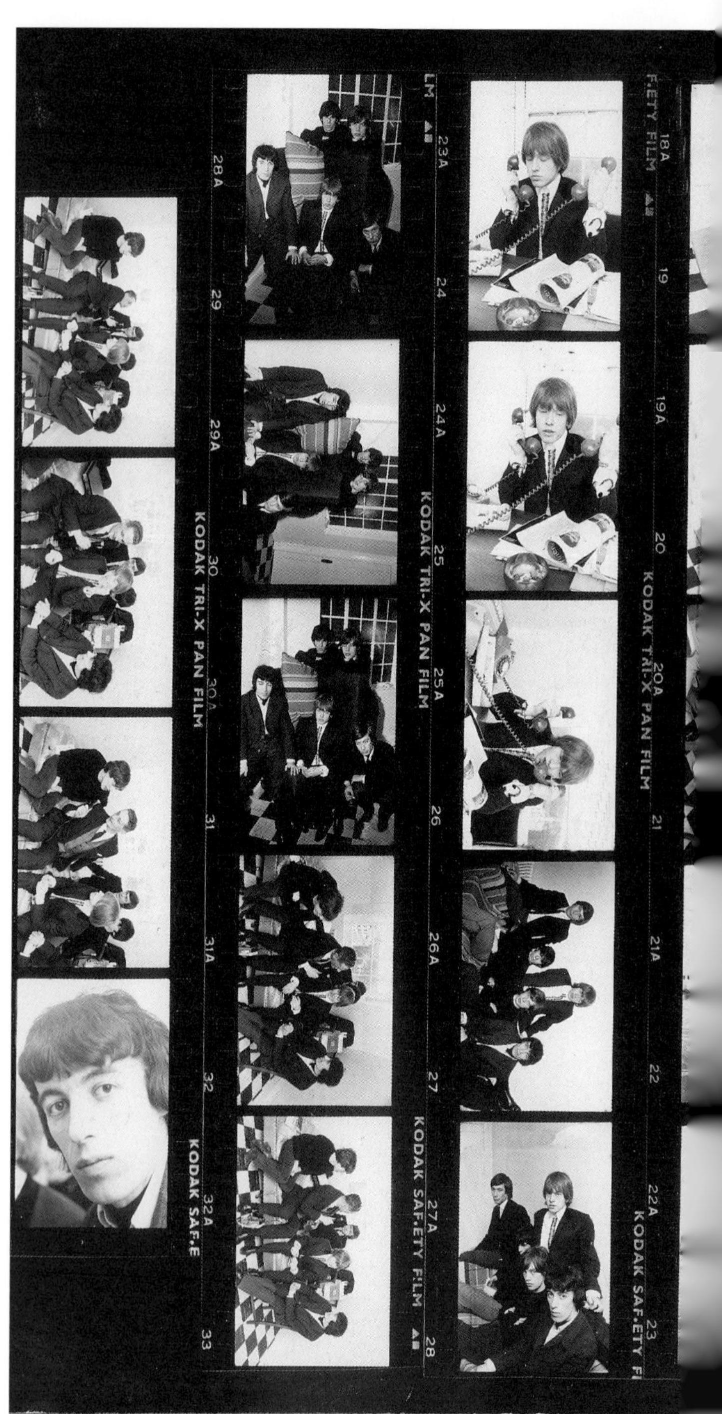


PHOTO SHOOT OF THE ROLLING STONES AT **IVOR COURT**

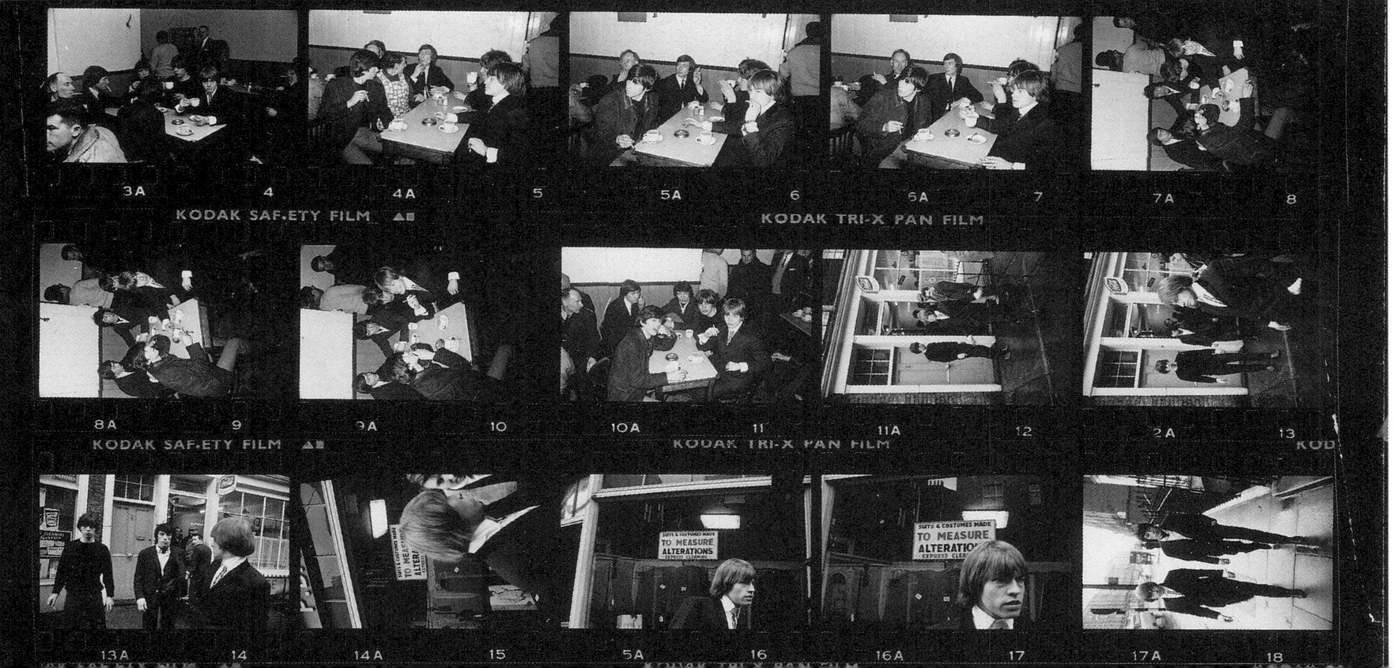

3A 4 4A 5 5A 6 6A 7 7A 8
KODAK SAF.ETY FILM
KODAK TRI-X PAN FILM
8A 9 9A 10 10A 11 11A 12 2A 13
KODAK SAF.ETY FILM
KODAK TRI-X PAN FILM
SUITS & COSTUMES MADE
TO MEASURE
ALTERATIONS
13A 14 14A 15 5A 16 16A 17 17A 18

**17** | Where: 138 Ivor Court, Gloucester Place
Who: **THE ROLLING STONES**
When: 1963-1964

The Rolling Stones' first manager, Andrew Oldham, established the group's management offices in his flat. It was here that Oldham set their dangerous image with the question, "Would you let your daughter marry a Rolling Stone?"

**18** | Where: Baker Street
When: 1978

**GERRY RAFFERTY** wrote his first solo hit single, *Baker Street*, when he was staying with friends on Baker Street.

Rafferty, from Paisley in Scotland, had been in several groups and had chart success with *Stuck In The Middle With You* whilst in the group, Stealers Wheel.

*Baker Street* was his second single as a solo artist. Further singles did not reach its success.

And...

**THE JAM** used Baker Street Underground Station for the cover of their single, *Down In The Tube Station At Midnight*.

**19** | Where: Marylebone Road, Madame Tussauds

This world-famous waxworks' museum has on show the figures of many Rock & Pop Stars of London.

**20** | Where: Marylebone Road, Royal Academy Of Music
When: 1958 & 1971

**ELTON JOHN** won a scholarship in 1958 to the Royal Academy of Music and attended piano classes every Saturday for a year: "I never enjoyed the lessons. It was a bore and I didn't like practising."

In 1997 Elton was honoured with a Fellowship of the Academy: "It just goes to show you what comes of not practising," he said.

Also...

**ANNIE LENNOX** of The Eurythmics came down from Scotland in 1971 on a scholarship to the college when she was seventeen. But she was disillusioned by the institution and soon left to write her own music, supporting herself as a waitress in Camden.

**21** | Where: 27-50 Marylebone Road, Harley House
Who: **MICK JAGGER-THE ROLLING STONES**
When: 1966

Mick Jagger lived at Harley House for a year before moving to Cheyne Walk. Long-term girlfriend Marianne Faithfull moved in with him when ex-girlfriend Chrissie Shrimpton moved out after a suicide attempt. Jagger rented the flat for £50 a week.

According to Faithfull, Jagger led an abstemious lifestyle, declining drugs and preferring to read rather than orgy in bed. A contrast to the image he portrayed of himself.

**22** | Where: 2 Park Square Mews, Upper Harley Street
Who: **JOHN PEEL & T REX**
When: Early 1969

The Radio One DJ John Peel has been influential for over thirty years in promoting new bands and music. From Marc Bolan through The Faces, to Punk and The Smiths, many groups have reached a popular audience for the first time on his show.

And...

**T REX**'s third album *Unicorn* was the group's first chart success and Peel had helped the band by featuring them on his radio shows. The photograph for the cover was shot at Peel's home.

**23** | Where: Euston Road, Euston Centre
When: 1970s

**SUPERTRAMP** recorded the album *Crisis? What Crisis?* in the Scorpio Studios at the centre in 1975. They ran out of material during the session and so had to write new songs, including *Ain't Nobody But Me*, in the studio.

And...

**THE SEX PISTOLS** notoriously appeared on the 'Today' show with Bill Grundy on 1 December 1976 in the Thames Television Studios to promote their debut single *Anarchy In The UK*. Grundy disliked the group and provoked them into swearing. Amongst the obscenities uttered by the group were "you dirty fucker". The programme caused outrage; one viewer reportedly put his foot through his TV in disgust. Grundy was fired and The Sex Pistols got the biggest publicity boost of their career.

**24** | Where: 26 Carburton Street
Who: **BOY GEORGE**
When: 1979-1980

Boy George squatted in this house with the singer Marilyn, prior to the formation of Culture Club. George spent his days here developing his early geisha-girl style.

His experimentation with clothes at this time was tested at the Trooping of the Colour in May 1981 when he dressed up as Queen Boadicea in front of Buckingham Palace.

**25** | Where: 35 Portland Place, IBC Studios
When: 1960s

**THE KINKS** recorded their first No.1 hit *You Really Got Me* in July 1964 at the Studios. The song was recorded with two session players: Jimmy Page (later of Led Zeppelin) on guitar and Jon Lord (Deep Purple) on organ.

Also...

**THE WHO** recorded *My Generation* and in 1968 *Tommy* at IBC. Whilst recording *Tommy*, the group had to perform at weekends to pay for studio time.

**26** | Where: 96 Portland Place, Flat 20
Who: **CILLA BLACK**
When: Late 1960s

Cilla Black lived in this flat, conveniently close to the BBC Radio studios, where she and other music stars often worked.

Born in Liverpool, she was spotted singing at the Cavern Club by The Beatles' manager, Brian Epstein. As friends, The Beatles were frequent visitors to her flat.

**57 WIMPOLE STREET** HOME TO PAUL MCCARTNEY FOR SEVERAL YEARS

**27** | Where: 57 Wimpole Street
Who: **PAUL McCARTNEY-THE BEATLES**
When: 1963-1966

Paul McCartney lived at the home of girlfriend Jane Asher's parents for about three years when The Beatles moved down to London in 1963. He was given his own room on the top floor at the back of the house. Asher's father was a doctor and her mother a professor at the Guildhall School of Music.

*I Wanna Hold Your Hand* was written here by McCartney for Jane Asher. It was recorded in October 1963 and became The Beatles' first US No.1.

McCartney also wrote *Yesterday* here:

> "I had a piano by my bedside and I must have dreamed it, because I tumbled out of bed and put my hands on the piano keys and I had a tune in my head. It was just all there, a complete thing. I couldn't believe it. It came too easy. In fact, I didn't believe I had written it. I thought maybe I heard it before, it was some other tune, and I went around for weeks playing the chords of the song for people, asking them - is this like something? I *think* I've written it."

First released in 1965, *Yesterday* has been recorded by over 600 other artists.

McCartney moved out when he bought his own house in Cavendish Avenue, St John's Wood in 1966.

**28** | Where: 99-100 Marylebone High Street, Cecil House
Who: **CLIFF RICHARD**
When: Late 1950s

As he was breaking into the music world of London, Cliff Richard shared a flat in this block, with his backing group, The Shadows.

**29** | Where: 22 Manchester Street
Who: **MARC BOLAN**
When: 1966

Marc Bolan was living in Manchester Street when he met Simon Napier-Bell. Napier-Bell was a successful manager of The Yardbirds and other groups, and agreed to manage Bolan in the band, John's Children.

During this time, Bolan's writing was strongly influenced by Tolkein and Bob Dylan. His glam-rock style of music was yet to develop.

**30** | Where: 39 Manchester Street
Who: **DAVID BOWIE**
When: June 1967-Spring 1968

This was the home of Kenneth Pitt, David Bowie's manager at the start of his solo career. Bowie lived with Pitt in Manchester Street when his debut album *David Bowie* was released in the summer of 1967.

**31** | Where: 94 Baker Street, Apple Boutique
Who: **THE BEATLES**
When: 5 December 1967-31 July 1968

Apple Boutique was the fashion venture of The Beatles' company, Apple Corps Ltd. Originally the building had huge colourful murals on its walls but these were painted over when neighbouring shops won a court injunction.

Though massively popular, the enterprise was so badly run that it had to close after seven months.

**32** | Where: 20 Manchester Square, EMI House
When: February 1963 & August 1995

**THE BEATLES** stood leaning over the stairwell of EMI House for the famous photograph by Angus McBean. The photograph, taken in February 1963, appeared on the cover of *Please Please Me* and the first of their two compilation albums, *The Beatles 1962-1966*. In May 1969, McBean again photographed The Beatles in the same place and this was used on the second compilation album, *The Beatles 1967-1970*.

And...

**BLUR** had a publicity photo taken on 5 August 1995 in exactly the same pose.

Blur's record company, Food (Records) Ltd, is based in Camden at 17A Arlington Road, NW1.

EMI moved from Manchester Square to Brook Green, W6 on 2 August 1995.

**33** | Where: 309 Regent Street, Polytechnic Of Central London
Who: **PINK FLOYD**
When: 1965-1967

Richard Wright, Roger Waters and Nick Mason of Pink Floyd met when studying architecture here. The three students formed the group Sigma 6 and shared a flat in Highgate. They left the college in February 1967 to play professionally.

Pink Floyd formed when Sigma 6 joined up with Syd Barrett. He was an old friend of Waters from Cambridge and was studying at Camberwell Art College in South London. Waters and Barrett had been neighbours and went to Cambridge High School for Boys, now Hills Road VI Form College, in the early 1960s.

**34** | Where: 48 Margaret Street, Speakeasy Club
When: 1960s & 1970s

**DAVID BOWIE** met his future wife, Angie Barnet, an American design student, on 9 April 1969 at this club. He was at the party to celebrate the launch of the group, King Crimson, whose guitarist, Robert Fripp, later played on Bowie's song *Heroes*.

And...

**DEEP PURPLE** played their first gig at the club on 10 July 1969 with new members Roger Glover and Ian Gillan.

And...

**THIN LIZZY** was formed in Dublin by Phil Lynott and Brian Downey. They debuted in England here in December 1970 playing Jimi Hendrix songs. It was not a success and the band had to wait until 1973 before achieving chart recognition.

And...

**THE NEW YORK DOLLS'** drummer, Billy Murcia, spent his last night at the club before dying on 6 November 1972 of drug abuse.

His death inspired the lyrics of David Bowie's song *Time*: *"Time ... in Quaaludes and red wine/ demanding Billy Dolls and other friends of mine."*

Also...

**PETE TOWNSHEND** met The Sex Pistols in February 1979 at the club. Townshend, depressed and drunk, told them that they were the only hope for rock. A photographer tried to capture the conversation and ended up in a fight with Townshend.

Later Townshend fell asleep on the pavement outside. He was woken by a policeman the next morning and sent home. The night's events inspired Townshend to write The Who's single, *Who Are You?*.

**35** | Where: John Princes Street, London College Of Fashion
Who: **BANANARAMA**
When: 1980

Siobhan Fahey and Sarah Dallin met on a journalism course here. They played in the band, The Professionals, with Paul Cook of The Sex Pistols and rehearsed in his flat in nearby Denmark Street, squashed between No.s 6 & 8.

Siobhan Fahey eventually left Bananarama to form Shakespeare's Sister and married Dave Stewart from The Eurythmics.

Pink Floyd playing at the **UFO Club** in 1967

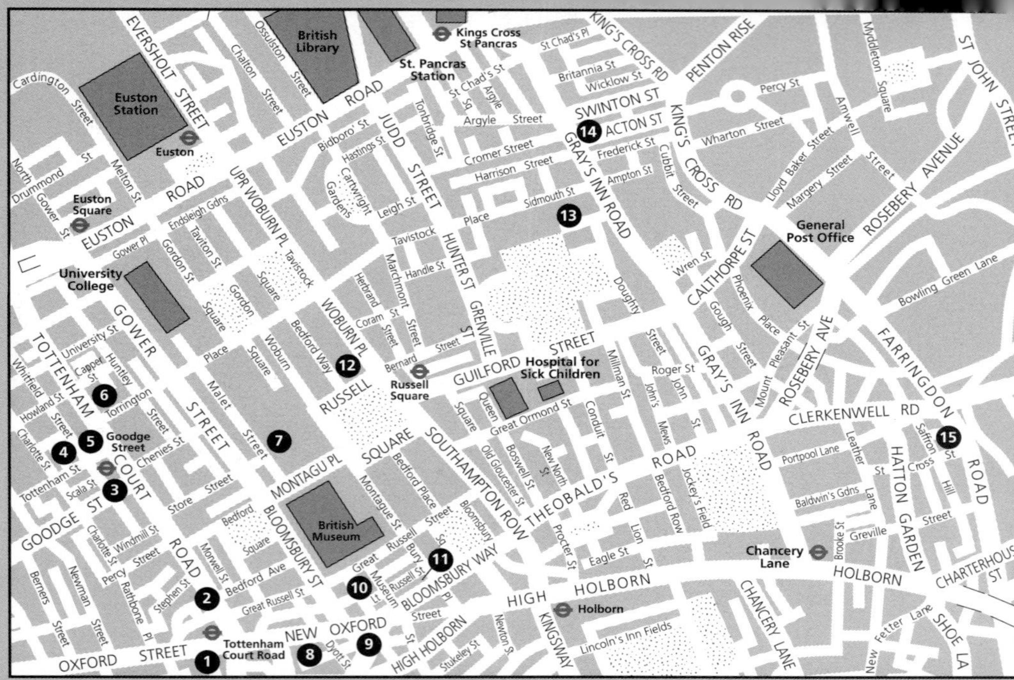


Central London Tottenham Court Road W1 & Bloomsbury WC1 | EC1

# Tottenham Court Road W1

**1** | Where: Tottenham Court Road Tube Station
Who: **DAVID BOWIE**
When: Early 1972

Bowie created the Ziggy Stardust character based on Vince Taylor, an eccentric musician, who performed outside this tube station.

He first staged the Ziggy character at Lancaster Arts Festival in February 1972, with his band, The Spiders from Mars. Ziggy Stardust 'died' at the Hammersmith Odeon on 3 July 1973 at the end of Bowie's 1973 UK tour.

**2** | Where: 31 Tottenham Court Road, UFO Club
When: 1960s

**PINK FLOYD** became the house band at Britain's first psychedelic club from December 1966 to October 1967. Here, the group developed their set into a mix of colour and images, whilst they remained anonymous behind the music.

During the day, the UFO reverted to an Irish Club called The Blaney.

Also...

**PROCOL HARUM** played their second live gig at the UFO in December 1967 on the day *A Whiter Shade Of Pale* was released.

Procol Harum was formed in 1967 by Gary Brooker and lyricist Keith Reid.

**3** | Where: 68 Tottenham Court Road, Church Of Scientology
Who: **VAN MORRISON**
When: 1985

Van Morrison taught part-time at the church when he converted to Scientology. It was at this time that he became interested in traditional Celtic music, particularly that of his native Ireland. Morrison began his music career with Them, from 1963 to their split in 1966. He then began a solo career with the hit *Brown-eyed Girl*. He now lives in Holland Park, West London.

**4** | Where: 58 Charlotte Street, Scala Theatre
Who: **THE BEATLES**
When: 31 March 1964

The Scala Theatre was used in the film, 'A Hard Day's Night'. The scene was the group performing on a television show. In the audience as a film extra was the young Phil Collins.

'A Hard Day's Night' was a great influence throughout the world, inspiring people to write music and form bands. Most of the locations for the film were in and around London.

**5** | Where: 31-37 Whitfield Street, CBS Studios
Who: **THE CLASH**
When: January 1977

The Clash had their first ever recording session at the studios after signing a recording contract with CBS. The result was their debut album *The Clash*, recorded over only three weekends. From the album came their first single *White Riot*.

The studio has since been demolished.

**6** | Where: 164-166 Tottenham Court Road, Regent Sound Studios
Who: **THE BEATLES**
When: 9 February 1967

The Beatles' first recording session outside Abbey Road took place here, when their usual studios were fully booked.

In two sessions, they recorded *Fixing A Hole* for the *Sergeant Pepper* album. Paul McCartney said the song referred to repairs he was making at his Scottish farmhouse on the Isle of Mull. However, amongst the many rumours at the time, was one that it referred to heroin-use.

## Bloomsbury WC1|EC1

**7** | Where: Malet Street, University of London Union
Who: **THE SMITHS**
When: 6 May 1983

At this early London gig, The Smiths, fresh from Manchester, were spotted by John Walters, the producer of John Peel's Radio One show. From this meeting, the group recorded the notable 'Smiths Sessions' for his late-night radio show. These sessions were instrumental in the success of The Smiths.

**8** | Where: 71-75 New Oxford Street, Dick James Music
Who: **ELTON JOHN**
When: June 1967

Here, Elton John met lyricist Bernie Taupin after they had corresponded for several months. The following year, they both became staff writers for Dick James Music (early Beatles' publishers):

> "It was ridiculous how many people were making demos up at Dick James' studio, but one day he discovered what was going on... "Who the hell are Reg Dwight and Bernie Taupin?" he shouted, and ... so we signed with Dick James as songwriters."

Dick James died in February 1986 from a heart-attack, just after Elton John, Taupin and John Reid (John's manager) had won a court case for unpaid royalties. Dick James' family blamed his death on the court case.

Cat Stevens outside his father's restaurant, **The Moulin Rouge**

**9** | Where: 49 New Oxford Street, Moulin Rouge
Who: **CAT STEVENS**
When: 21 July 1947

Cat Stevens, born Steven Demetri Georigiou, lived during his childhood in the flat above his father's restaurant, the Moulin Rouge. After school (Northampton Secondary Modern in Old Street) and at weekends, he worked in the kitchen of the restaurant.

It was whilst working at the restaurant that he wrote *Father and Son*.

**10** | Where: 35 Little Russell Street, Matrix Studios
When: 1979-1980

**MARIANNE FAITHFULL** recorded her album *Broken English* in this studio in 1979.

And…

**ADAM & THE ANTS** recorded *Antmusic* at Matrix Studios in April 1980. This was the group's first recording with Siouxsie & The Banshees' guitarist, Marco Pirroni. As a result of *Antmusic*, Adam & The Ants were offered a record deal with CBS in July of the same year.

**11** | Where: 7 Bury Place, Radha Krishna Temple
Who: **GEORGE HARRISON**
When: 1969

The monks of the Hare Krishna temple recorded with George Harrison on his record *Hare Krishna Mantra* that reached No.12 in the UK charts. Harrison gave money to help lease the building as a temple. They have since moved on.

**12** | Where: 38-52 Woburn Place, Royal Hotel
Who: **THE BEATLES**
When: 31 December 1961

The Beatles stayed at the Royal Hotel the night before their audition at Decca Records in West Hampstead. The group drove down from Liverpool in a small van and spent New Year's Eve at Trafalgar Square. However the audition was not a success.

When The Beatles first hit the charts and began to work in London, they lived in various hotels around the city. The Hotel President on Russell Square and the Royal Court Hotel on Sloane Square were just two.

In these early days The Beatles were inseparable, with Lennon and McCartney writing songs together.

Lennon remembers writing *Michelle*:

> "Paul walked in and hummed the first few bars with the words and he says 'where do I go from here?' I had been listening to Nina Simone - I think it was *I Put A Spell On You* - there was a line in it that went, 'I love you, I love you, I love you'. That's what made me think of the middle eight for *Michelle*. *'I love you, I love you, I lo-o-o-ove you.'* "

McCartney says of this period: "At least the first forty songs we wrote were Buddy Holly influenced."

**13** | Where: 45 Sidmouth Street, Kingsway College
Who: **THE SEX PISTOLS**
When: September 1973

John Lydon, later known as Johnny Rotten, came to Kingsway College after leaving St William of York Roman Catholic Secondary School (opposite Pentonville Prison) which he described as "a dungeon".

Lydon met Jah Wobble, in the enrolment queue at Kingsway. After the demise of The Sex Pistols, Lydon formed Public Image Limited with Wobble.

**14** | Where: 328 Grays Inn Road, The Water Rats
When: 1960s-present

**BOB DYLAN** appeared at the pub in December 1962 in a short folk performance, before he became famous. The pub was then called the Pindar of Wakefield.

And...

**THE POGUES** played their debut gig here in October 1982. Shane McGowan of The Pogues used to work in the Griffin pub in Villiers Street off Trafalgar Square.

And...

**OASIS** played their first headline gig at the Water Rats in 1994 and caught the attention of the music press.

**15** | Where: 91 Saffron Hill, Roundhouse Studios
Who: **AC/DC**
When: January 1979

AC/DC recorded *Highway to Hell* at these studios. (It was later mixed at Basing Street Studios.) *Highway to Hell* became the group's first top ten album.

The following year, singer Bon Scott died after a night of heavy drinking. He was found dead in a car outside a friend's house at 67 Overhill Road, in Dulwich, South-east London. Brian Johnson replaced him.

The Rolling Stones playing **Hyde Park** in July 1969

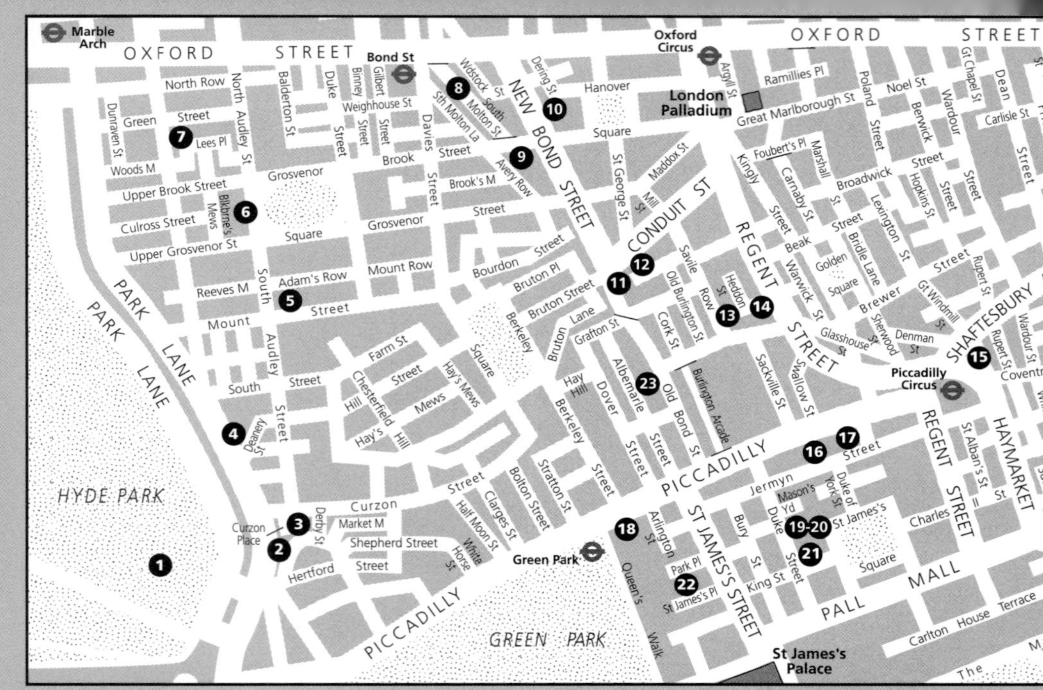
Marble Arch
OXFORD STREET
Bond St
Oxford Circus
London Palladium
North Row
North Audley St
Green Street
Dunraven St
Lees Pl
Woods M
Upper Brook Street
Bilkbrne's Mews
Culross Street
Upper Grosvenor St
Balderton St
Duke Street
Binney Street
Gilbert Street
Weighhouse St
Davies Street
Brook Street
Brook's M
Grosvenor Square
Grosvenor Street
Adam's Row
South Street
South Audley Street
Reeves M
Mount Row
Mount Street
PARK LANE
Deanery St
Farm St
Chesterfield Hill
Hay's Mews
Hay's Hill
Berkeley Square
Bourdon Street
Bruton Pl
Bruton Street
Bruton Lane
Grafton St
Wdstock St
Sth Molton La
South Molton St
NEW BOND STREET
Avery Row
Dering St
Hanover Square
St George St
Maddox St
Mill St
CONDUIT ST
Savile Row
Old Burlington St
Cork St
Heddon St
REGENT STREET
Kingly St
Foubert's Pl
Marshall St
Carnaby St
Ramillies Pl
Great Marlborough St
Poland Street
Noel St
Berwick Street
Wardour Street
Gt Chapel St
Dean Street
Carlisle St
Frith Street
Soho St
Broadwick Street
Hopkins St
Lexington St
Bridle Lane
Golden Square
Beak Street
Warwick St
Glasshouse St
Sherwood St
Denman St
Brewer Street
Gt Windmill St
Rupert St
SHAFTESBURY AVE
Wardour St
Coventry St
Whitcomb St
Piccadilly Circus
Albemarle Street
Dover Street
Berkeley Street
Hay Hill
Old Bond St
Burlington Arcade
Sackville St
Swallow St
PICCADILLY
Jermyn Street
Mason's Yd
Duke of York St
Duke Street
Bury St
St James's Square
Charles St
St Alban's St
HAYMARKET
Suffolk St
Arlington St
Park Pl
St James's Pl
ST JAMES'S STREET
King St
PALL MALL
Carlton House Terrace
The Mall
St James's Palace
Queen's Walk
GREEN PARK
Green Park
HYDE PARK
Curzon Place
Derby St
Curzon Street
Market M
Shepherd Street
Hertford Street
White Horse St
Half Moon St
Clarges St
Bolton Street
Stratton St
1
2
3
4
5
6
7
8
9
10
11
12
13
14
15
16
17
18
19-20
21
22
23

# Mayfair W1|SW1

**1** | Where: Hyde Park
When: Late 1960s

**PINK FLOYD** gave London's largest free concert on 29 June 1968 to promote their new album *A Saucerful Of Secrets*. The concert helped to revive Pink Floyd during a low period after Syd Barrett left the group in April 1968.

Also...

**THE ROLLING STONES** on 5 July 1969 played their free concert to over 250,000 people by the Serpentine Lake in the park. Three days before, their sacked guitarist Brian Jones had died and the concert was dedicated to his memory. Mick Jagger, wearing a dress, read Shelly's *'Adonias'* and released thousands of butterflies into the sky.

Jones' replacement, Mick Taylor, made his public debut with the group at this concert.

**2** | Where: Park Lane, Hilton International Hotel
When: Late 1960s-1970s

**THE BEATLES** attended a lecture by Maharishi Mahesh Yogi at the Hilton Hotel on 24 August 1967. They were introduced to the guru by George Harrison's wife, Patti Boyd.

Later, The Beatles went on a retreat to India with the guru. John Lennon wrote *Sexy Sadie* after becoming disillusioned with the guru's manipulation and sexual advances made to the sister of Mia Farrow.

Also…

**SYD BARRETT** lived in a penthouse suite at the Hilton from 1972-1974, several years after leaving Pink Floyd. Large royalties from the group's record sales ensured Barrett an income.

During this time, Barrett became a cult legend, occasionally performing at clubs in London, like the Middle Earth in Covent Garden.

Between leaving the Hilton in 1974 and returning to Cambridge, he lived in a modest flat at Chelsea Cloisters on Sloane Avenue, SW3.

**3** | Where: 9 Curzon Place
When: 1970s

**MAMA CASS** (real name Cass Elliot) of The Mamas and The Papas died in a flat in this block of serviced apartments after a concert in July 1974. The flat was leased to the singer Harry Nilsson at the time.

And…

**KEITH MOON**, drummer with The Who, died in the same flat on 7 September 1978.

Moon had spent the evening with Paul and Linda McCartney at a Buddy Holly Convention party, before going to the flat of his girlfriend, Annette Walter-Lax. Unable to sleep he took an accidental and fatal overdose of sedatives.

Moon used to lived in Chertsey, but sold his house, Tara, in 1974 to Kevin Godley, ex-10CC. It was at Tara that he expanded his 'Moon the Loon' legend: ordering a helicopter to fly him to the pub at the end of his drive; parking his Rolls Royce in the swimming pool; and holding manic 24-hour, seven-days-a-week parties.

Several months after his death in January 1979, Kenny Jones, ex-Small Faces and The Faces, replaced Moon and made his debut with The Who at the Rainbow Theatre, Finsbury Park in May.

**4** | Where: Park Lane, Dorchester Hotel
Who: **JOHN LENNON-THE BEATLES**
When: 6 July 1964 & 1969

Foyle's, the book shop on Charing Cross Road, held a literary luncheon at the Dorchester in honour of John Lennon's book, 'In His Own Write'. The cream of literary London waited to hear some of his famed wit. Unfortunately Lennon had drunk a lot the night before and he had not prepared a speech beyond, "Thank you very much". The lunch was not a success.

In early 1969, in the Art Deco Room of the hotel, Lennon met The Rolling Stones' manager, the American Allen Klein.

Lennon wanted to leave The Beatles and to extricate himself from both The Beatles' Apple Corporation and his long-time record company EMI.

Within half an hour of meeting Klein, Lennon wrote to the chairman of EMI: "Dear Sir Joe, from now on Allen Klein handles my stuff".

On the 3rd February 1969, Klein was appointed manager of The Beatles. Paul McCartney opposed Klein's appointment, leading to decades of acrimonious litigation.

**5** | Where: 18 Mount Street, Flat 23
Who: **KEITH RICHARDS-THE ROLLING STONES**
When: Autumn 1968

Keith Richards stayed at the home of friend and art dealer, Robert Fraser, during the shooting of the film 'Performance'. The film starred his girlfriend, Anita Pallenburg, and Mick Jagger.

Richards wrote much of the *Let It Bleed* album here. The references he made to the occult, drugs and violence became dominant themes for The Stones, mirroring the increasing turmoil in their personal lives.

Fraser had been arrested at Richards' Sussex house, Redlands, in February 1967, along with Richards and Jagger. He was the only one to serve a sentence when he pleaded guilty to possession of heroin. Fraser now runs an antiques shop in Vigo Street, W1.

**6** | Where: 24 Grosvenor Square, United States Embassy
Who: **MICK JAGGER-THE ROLLING STONES**
When: Spring 1968

Mick Jagger was innocently signing autographs in his Bentley as riots began at nearby Grosvenor Square. American Oxford University student, Bill Clinton, was amongst those demonstrating against war in Vietnam as was Malcolm McLaren (later manager of The Sex Pistols), who was setting fire to the US flag on the Roosevelt memorial.

The riots inspired Jagger to write *Street Fighting Man*, the first words of which he scribbled down as he was driven safely away: "... the time is right for fighting in the street ...".

**7** | Where: 57 Green Street, Flats L & I
Who: **GEORGE HARRISON & RINGO STARR**
When: Autumn 1963-Spring 1964

The Beatles stayed in Flat L when they moved to London. Paul McCartney and John Lennon stayed here for only a month, moving out in November.

Ringo Starr and George Harrison continued to share a flat here and moved to the smaller Flat I. They left shortly afterwards when fans discovered the address.

**8** | Where: 64 South Molton Street, Mayfair Sound Studio
When: 1960s & 1970s

**CREAM** recorded their second single *I Feel Free* here in September 1966. The song was written by Jack Bruce and Pete Brown.

And...

**GARY GLITTER**'s Glittersound was developed during a recording session at the studio in 1971. With arranger and composer Mike Leander (died May 1996), he recorded *Rock And Roll*, his first single under the name Gary Glitter. It was completed in 24 hours and stayed at No.2 in the UK charts for three weeks.

Glitter lived in York Street, north of Oxford Street, at this time. His previous manager, Vic Billings, lived nearby in Bryanston Square, and it was at his house that the name Gary Glitter was thought up.

Glitter's real name was Paul Gadd and he had been recording unsuccessfully as Paul Raven since 1960.

Mike Leander was a prolific producer and had worked with Marianne Faithfull in the late 1960s. Faithfull attributes her survival at the depth of drug addiction to Leander. He found her on the streets in Soho and provided a record contract and a flat in Bloomsbury.

**9** | Where: 25 Brook Street
Who: **JIMI HENDRIX**
When: January 1969-1970

Jimi Hendrix lived with girlfriend, Cathy Etchingham, in a flat above the restaurant, Mr Love. Whilst living here, Hendrix wrote the song *Little Wing* for her.

JIMI HENDRIX'S FLAT IN **BROOK STREET**

Also...
The eighteenth century German composer, George Frederic Handel, lived and died here.

**10** | Where: 73 & 104 New Bond Street, Levy's Studios
Who: **PAUL SIMON**
When: May 1965

Paul Simon's first solo album *The Paul Simon Song Book* was recorded here with one microphone for £60 per hour. Not long after the album was released *The Sound Of Silence* charted in the US and Simon returned to reform his duo with Art Garfunkel.

**11** | Where: 22 New Bond Street, London Arts Gallery
Who: **JOHN LENNON**
When: January 1970

John Lennon had a show of his erotic drawings of Yoko Ono at this gallery. Eight of the lithographs were confiscated for being obscene. This led to a court case, during which examples of Picasso's pictures were used and the charges were dropped.

**12** | Where: 38 Conduit Street, Westbury Hotel
Who: **JERRY LEE LEWIS**
When: May 1958

Jerry Lee Lewis was staying in Room 127 of the Westbury Hotel when the scandal of his marriage to Myra Gale Brown became public.

Britain was outraged by the third marriage of Lewis to his 13 year old cousin: not only was her age a problem, but he was still married to his second wife, Jane Mitcham.

Lewis changed from a headline act to being virtually unemployable. The last concert he played, before being shouted off stage, was at the Granada Theatre, Mitcham Road in Tooting.

John Lennon said of Lewis: "No-one, be it The Beatles, Dylan or The Stones, has ever improved on *Whole Lotta Shakin* for my money."

**13** | Where: 3 Savile Row, Apple Studios
Who: **THE BEATLES**
When: 30 January 1969

Headquarters of The Beatles' Apple Corporation.

The building had previously been the Albany gambling club and during the early 19th century it was the home of Admiral Lord Nelson and his mistress, Lady Hamilton.

Apple Corps was created to administer new projects. Financed by the need to offset a £2 million tax bill, The Beatles invited anyone with an idea to apply for backing. The result was a stampede and the building became a magnet for every type of creative endeavour, viable or not. Of the company's more successful ventures, the launching of James Taylor and Badfinger were probably the most famous. In the basement a state-of-the-art studio was built where The Beatles tried to record tracks for the *Let It Be* album. But the studio was unworkable and the sessions had to be moved to Twickenham.

THE ROOFTOP OF **3 SAVILE ROW** WHERE THE BEATLES LAST PERFORMED LIVE

The Beatles performed together for the last time on the roof of the building, playing *Get Back*, in January 1969. They played for only 40 minutes before the Royal Bank of Scotland, opposite, complained to the police.

**14** | Where: Heddon Street
Who: **DAVID BOWIE**
When: January 1972

The photograph for the cover of *The Rise And Fall Of Ziggy Stardust And The Spiders From Mars* was taken here.

**15** | Where: 3 Piccadilly Circus, Rock Circus
Who: **THE BEATLES**
When: 17 July 1968

Rock Circus, a waxworks museum for the world of Rock and Pop, is housed in the London Pavilion.

The last demonstration of Beatlemania was at the Pavilion, during the premier of the Beatles' 1968 film, 'The Yellow Submarine'. Their previous film, 'A Magical Mystery Tour', was not a critical success despite a TV audience of 15 million.

The Pavilion was also the setting for premiers of the previous Beatles' films, 'A Hard Day's Night' and 'Help!'.

**16** | Where: 181 Piccadilly, Fortnum & Mason's Tea Room
Who: **ADAM FAITH**
When: 1970s-1990s

Adam Faith used the table opposite the entrance of the restaurant as a base for the Faith Corporation, a financial advisory company in the 1980s. The table was permanently reserved for him and a telephone extension added.

Born as Terence Nelhams in West London, he lived in Churchfield Road East whilst attending John Perring Junior and Acton Wells Schools.

Faith was discovered singing at the 2i's Coffee Bar in Compton Street, W1, in July 1955 by impresario, Larry Parnes.

In the 1970s he discovered and managed Leo Sayer; in the 1990s he returned to acting.

**17** | Where: 201 Piccadilly, Command Studios
Who: **ROXY MUSIC**
When: 1 March 1972

The group's debut album *Roxy Music* was recorded here. Further albums were also recorded at the studios.

The motorbike sound at the beginning of *Virginia Plain* was recorded from a bike riding up and down Piccadilly. The song was Roxy Music's first single and established them as a leading art-rock band.

Bryan Ferry was the singer and songwriter and he named the group after his favourite cinema, the Roxy in Brixton.

Ferry attended art school in Newcastle before teaching pottery at St Paul's School for Girls in Hammersmith. He held a couple of art exhibitions, one at the Piccadilly Gallery, 16A Cork Street, near the studios, before opting for a musical career.

**18** | Where: Piccadilly, Ritz Hotel
Who: **MICK JAGGER-THE ROLLING STONES**
When: December 1978-January 1979

Mick Jagger wrote *Start Me Up* whilst staying at the Ritz. This was during The Stones' tax-exile years, in which he was not allowed to live at his house on Cheyne Walk. The song was released as the first single from the *Tattoo You* album of 1981. Jagger and Keith Richards were not getting along well at this time: Richards was in the depth of his heroin addiction which began after the death of his young son in 1976, whilst Jagger enjoyed social success and a new life with the model Jerry Hall.

*Start Me Up* put The Stones at the top of the US charts for the first time since 1973 and saw the return of their raw and aggressive sound of earlier years.

**19** | Where: 6 Mason's Yard, Indica Gallery
Who: **JOHN LENNON & YOKO ONO**
When: 9 November 1966

At the Indica Gallery, John Lennon met Yoko Ono for the first time. The gallery was owned by Barry Miles, Peter Asher and John Dunbar, the first husband of Marianne Faithfull. Dunbar lived at 11 Bentinck Mansions in Bentinck Street and

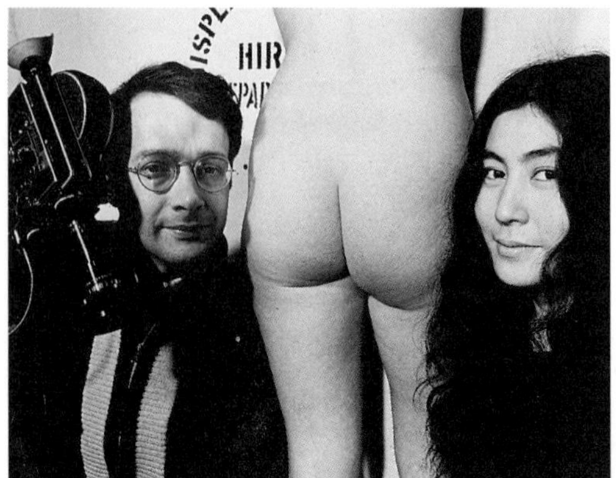

YOKO ONO AND HUSBAND TONY COX AT THE **INDICA GALLERY**

was a good friend of Paul McCartney. McCartney designed their wrapping paper.

Ono had been told that Lennon was a possible financial backer for her conceptual art works and so she had invited him to the opening of her exhibition, 'Unfinished Objects and Paintings' in November 1966.

When he arrived, she gave Lennon a piece of paper with the word 'BREATHE' on it. This was enough to get Lennon's interest.

Ono remembers the meeting:

> "Lennon asked if he could hammer a nail into my painting, 'Painting to Hammer A Nail In'. I told him it would cost five shillings - Lennon then asked if he could use an imaginary nail instead."

The affair developed with Lennon becoming increasingly influenced by her. Ono introduced him to a world of experimental art and music, which was to divert his attention from the more popular style of The Beatles.

**20** | Where: 13 Mason's Yard, Scotch Of St James
Who: **PAUL McCARTNEY**
When: 3 February 1966

Paul McCartney met Stevie Wonder for the first time at this popular 1960s night-club. Many years later, the two performed the song *Ebony And Ivory* together.

**21** | Where: 8 Duke Street, 11 Dalmeney Court
Who: **THE ANIMALS-ERIC BURDON**
When: October 1965-late 1966

Eric Burdon, lead singer of The Animals, lived at Dalmeney Court when the song *I'm Crying* was released. This was the first single that the group had written. Burdon wrote the song with Alan Price.

The original Animals split up in September 1966 due to Burdon's drug-taking and unreliability. For a time, he continued with a new line-up of The Animals.

**22** | Where: 7-8 Park Place, St James's Club
When: 1990s

David Bowie, Cher, Tina Turner and Robert Palmer are members of this private club.

**23** | Where: 11 Albemarle Street, Liberty Records
Who: **ELTON JOHN**
When: 17 June 1967

Liberty was an American record label. Elton John replied to their advertisement for recording artists. At the time he was doing session work and playing with Long John Baldry in Bluesology. He was frustrated and wanted to pursue a solo career:

> "Bluesology would never let me sing… I didn't really want to be lead singer. I just wanted to do backing vocals … 'Ooos' and 'Ahhhs'. But I wasn't really even allowed to do that."

John was invited to audition at the Regent Sound Studios, but failed to win a deal. However, he was given some lyrics sent to Liberty by Bernie Taupin. As a result, John corresponded with Taupin, leading several months later to their meeting and a partnership.

Jimi Hendrix playing at **the Marquee Club** on Wardour Street

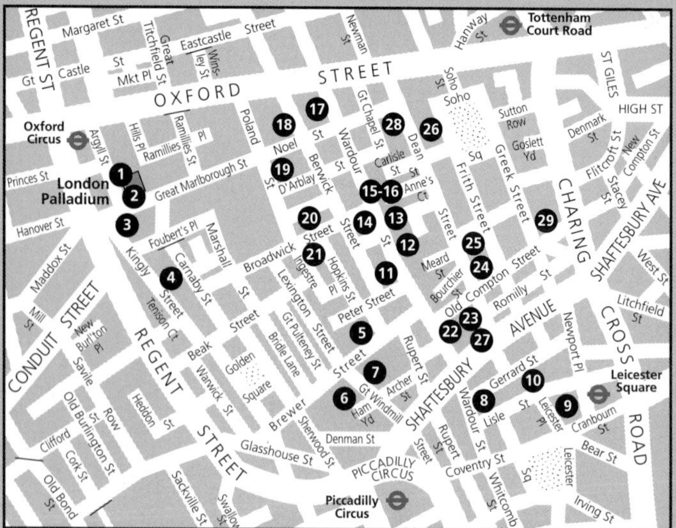

REGENT ST
Margaret St
Great Titchfield St
Eastcastle Street
Newman St
Hanway St
Tottenham Court Road
Gt Castle St
Mkt Pl
Winsley St
OXFORD STREET
Soho St
Soho Sq
ST GILES HIGH ST
Oxford Circus
Argyll St
Hills Pl
Ramillies Pl
Ramillies St
Poland St
Noel St
Gt Chapel St
Wardour St
Dean St
Sutton Row
Goslett Yd
Denmark St
Flitcroft St
New Compton St
Princes St
London Palladium
Great Marlborough St
D'Arblay St
Berwick Street
Carlisle St
St Anne's Ct
Frith Street
Greek Street
CHARING CROSS ROAD
Stacey St
SHAFTESBURY AVE
Hanover St
Foubert's Pl
Marshall St
Broadwick Street
Hopkins St
Meard St
Old Compton Street
Romilly St
West St
Maddox St
Kingly Street
Carnaby St
Ingestre Pl
Lexington Street
Peter Street
Bourchier St
Litchfield St
Mill St
CONDUIT STREET
New Burlington Pl
Tenison Ct
Beak Street
Gt Pulteney St
Bridle Lane
Rupert St
SHAFTESBURY AVENUE
Newport Pl
Savile Row
REGENT STREET
Golden Square
Warwick St
Archer St
Gerrard St
Leicester Square
Old Burlington St
Heddon St
Brewer St
Gt Windmill St
Ham Yd
Wardour St
Lisle St
Leicester Pl
Cranbourn St
Clifford St
Cork St
Sherwood St
Denman St
Bear St
Glasshouse St
PICCADILLY CIRCUS
Rupert St
Coventry St
Leicester Sq
Old Bond St
Sackville St
Swallow St
Piccadilly Circus
Whitcomb St
Irving St
1
2
3
4
5
6
7
8
9
10
11
12
13
14
15-16
17
18
19
20
21
22
23
24
25
26
27
28
29

# Soho W1

**1** | Where: 8 Argyll Street, The London Palladium
Who: **THE BEATLES**
When: 13 October 1963

The Beatles played a live TV performance at the Palladium for ITV's 'Sunday Night at the London Palladium'. The audience went wild and the next day, newspapers first used the term "Beatlemania".

**2** | Where: 5-6 Argyll Street, NEMS, Sutherland House
Who: **BRIAN EPSTEIN**
When: 1966-67

**THE BEATLES'** manager Brian Epstein had offices here in the mid-1960s. His company, NEMS, originally at 13 Monmouth Street, moved to larger premises when The Beatles, amongst other bands under his management, became successful.

It was here on 4 March 1966 that John Lennon conducted his famous interview with Maureen Cleeve of 'The Evening Standard' before the group's tour of the States. His comment that The Beatles were "more popular than Jesus" caused uproar in the US. Their effigies were burnt, their records were banned and the Klu Klux Klan threatened to lynch the group. The hysteria led directly to The Beatles giving up live performances after the tour finished at Candlewick Park.

Also...

THE LONDON PALLADIUM

**THE BEE GEES**, born in Liverpool but brought up in Australia, signed a management contract on 24 February 1967 in the NEMS offices with Robert Stigwood, who worked for Epstein.

The Bee Gees had auditioned at Epstein's Saville Theatre earlier on the same day. By October, they had their first hit *Massachusetts* and a house in Eaton Square.

Stigwood went on to produce the film 'Saturday Night Fever', starring John Travolta and with the soundtrack by The Bee Gees. Stigwood is also Australian. He arrived in London in 1959 with £3 and is today worth about £160 million, owning the rights to the film 'Grease'.

**3** | Where: 9 Kingly Street, Bag O'Nails
Who: **PAUL McCARTNEY-THE BEATLES**
When: 15 May 1967

Whilst watching Georgie Fame playing at this jazz club, Paul McCartney first met New York photographer, Linda Eastman. They met again two days later at Brian Epstein's party for the release of *Sergeant Pepper* album.

**4** | Where: Carnaby Street
When: 1960s

Carnaby Street became a fashion centre in the 1960s, and symbol of the phrase 'Swinging London'. Many boutiques were set up in the street by designers and retailers catering for the boom in youth fashion. Mary Quant's mini skirt first went on sale here.

Carnaby Street provided inspiration for The Kinks' satirical song, *Dedicated Follower Of Fashion*: *"Everywhere the Carnabation Army moves on"*.

The offices of Smash Hits magazine were at 52-55 Carnaby Street in the early 1980s. Neil Tennant was working there when he formed the Pet Shop Boys.

Boy George worked at a boutique on the street before his career in music.

**CARNABY STREET** IN THE 1960S ...

AND IN 1997

At the north end is Great Marlborough Street Magistrates Court where Brian Jones, Mick Jagger, Marianne Faithfull and Johnny Rotten have all appeared at one time.

**5** | Where: 10 Brewer Street, Jack Of Clubs
Who: **DAVID BOWIE**
When Late 1964

David Bowie, performing under his real name David Jones, played his first professional gig here with The King Bees. He was working for a design agency in Bond Street at the time.

The band played rhythm and blues and were paid £100. They stopped after just two songs due to the audience's lack of enthusiasm.

**6** | Where: Ham Yard, 14 Great Windmill Street, The Scene Club
When: 1963-64

**THE ANIMALS** played their first London gig at this venue, now a café, in December 1963. This was before they had recorded *House Of The Rising Sun*.

Also...

**THE WHO** were introduced to the world of mod culture revolving around The Scene Club in early 1964 as a means to promote themselves.

Originally called The Detours, the struggling group changed their name to The High Numbers and were given a mod image: 'High Numbers' was a mod term for 'style leader'. In July 1964 they released their first single *I'm The Face,* again a reference to someone of importance in the youth culture.

**7** | Where: Great Windmill Street
Who: **MARIANNE FAITHFULL**
When: Early 1970s

After leaving Mick Jagger and without a career, Marianne Faithfull spent several years in drug addiction. For some months she lived rough on the streets of Soho, with occasional visits to her mother and son in Reading. She passed her days on the church wall in Great Windmill Street, unrecognised and in a drugged stupor from one fix to another. Or on a wall in St Anne's Court, off Wardour Street, opposite her dealer's room over a restaurant.

**8** | Where: 33-37 Wardour Street, The Flamingo Club
Who: **GEORGIE FAME**
When: December 1961

Georgie Fame (born Clive Powell) and his band, The Blue Flames, gained popularity as the house band at this jazz club. They made the break from rock and roll to jazz, for which Georgie Fame is now better known.

Fame was discovered by his manager, Larry Parnes, and the songwriter, Lionel Bart, in October 1959, playing the piano in a London pub. For a while he was used to back the other acts managed by Parnes.

**9** | Where: 7 Leicester Place, Ad Lib Club
Who: **SIMON NAPIER-BELL**
When: 1966

Simon Napier-Bell co-wrote the Dusty Springfield hit song *You Don't Have To Say You Love Me* on the way to the club.

Napier-Bell subsequently managed several groups, including The Yardbirds, Japan and Wham!

The popular sixties club was where Ringo Starr proposed to his first wife, Maureen Cox.

**FLAMINGO &**
**ALLNIGHTER CLUBS**

33-37 Wardour Street, W.1.
Rik Gunnell and Tony Harris
present:

★ FRIDAY (13th) 8 - 11.30
SUNSPOTS

★ FRIDAY (13th) 12 - 5 a.m.
GEORGIE FAME
AND BLUE FLAMES
TONY SHEVETON
AND SHEVELLES

★ SATURDAY (14th) 7 - 11.30
DON RENDELL QUINTET
Ian Carr (Trumpet)
DICK MORRISSEY
QUARTET
HARRY SOUTH TRIO

★ SATURDAY (14th) 12 - 6 a.m.
GEORGIE FAME
AND BLUE FLAMES
DICK MORRISSEY
QUARTET
RONNIE SCOTT

★ SUNDAY (15th) Afternoon 3 - 6
TONY SHEVETON
AND SHEVELLES

★ SUNDAY (15th) 7.15 - 11 p.m.
TONY SHEVETON
AND SHEVELLES

★ MONDAY (16th) 8 - 1
GEORGIE FAME
AND BLUE FLAMES

☆ THURSDAY (19th) 8 - 1
DAVE DAVANI
THE 'D' MEN & BERYL

Poster advertising a gig at **the Flamingo Club**

**10** | Where: 39 Gerrard Street, Ronnie Scott's
When: Until late 1960s

This was the original site of the well-known jazz club, now located in Frith Street.

**11** | Where: 87 Wardour Street
Who: **PETE TOWNSHEND-THE WHO**
When: 1966

Pete Townshend, lead singer of The Who, lived in the top floor flat of this building in the mid-sixties. He converted part of the flat into a studio.

**12** | Where: 90 Wardour Street, The Marquee Club
When: mid-1960s

**THE WHO** changed their name from The High Numbers on the advice of their manager, Kit Lambert, and started playing on Tuesday nights at The Marquee's new Soho premises.

In early 1965, they wrote *Anyway Anyhow Anywhere*, the day before they were due to record their next single. It was the first song they recorded with distorted feedback, a result of the group's experiment with new sounds in the studio.

Also...

**DAVID BOWIE**, still known as David Jones, played here with The Lower Third, in September 1965.

The group were spotted by Kenneth Pitt and given a record deal with Pye. When The Lower Third broke up in February 1966, Bowie went solo.

And...

**PINK FLOYD** played at Sunday afternoon 'Spontaneous Underground' sessions in Spring 1966. They developed their psychedelic sound and abandoned blues/jazz music.

In May 1966, they were seen here by Peter Jenner, who became their manager, along with a friend Andrew King. Blackhill Enterprises was formed by Jenner and King with the members of Pink Floyd, to develop the group's music and light shows.

And...

**LED ZEPPELIN** played their first London gig at The Marquee on 16 October 1968 where they recorded their debut live LP. They were still called The New Yardbirds.

And...

**THE SEX PISTOLS**, on 14 February 1976, supported Eddie & The Hot Rods at the first punk festival to be held in London.

Neil Spencer of the NME wrote a review of the gig for the paper and used the phrase "punk rock" for the first time.

**13** | Where: 100 Wardour Street, La Chasse Club
Who: **YES**
When: May 1968

Yes formed when Jon Anderson and Chris Squire met at this club.

**14** | Where: 101 Wardour Street, Rocket Records
Who: **ELTON JOHN**
When: May 1973

After the successes of *Crocodile Rock* and *Daniel*, Elton John set up his own record label, Rocket Records. John intended the label to take on other artists. The greatest successes for Rocket were in the US with Cliff Richard's first top ten *Devil Woman*, Neil Sedaka's comeback in the mid-1970s and Kiki Dee. But the label's UK success rested with releases from John himself. Rocket Records is now part of Island Records.

*Song For Guy* was written in 1979 and dedicated to Guy Burchett, a Rocket Record errand boy who died when driving his motorbike on the way to the office.

**15** | Where: St Anne's Court, Wardour Street, Blue Gardenia Club
Who: **THE BEATLES**
When: 9 December 1961

The Beatles played their first London performance in this small club. The gig was a few weeks before their unsuccessful audition for Decca.

Only John Lennon and Paul McCartney had performed in the south of England before in 1960 at the Fox & Hounds Pub on Gosbrook Road in Caversham. The pub belonged to McCartney's cousin.

**16** | Where: 17 St Anne's Court, Wardour Street, Trident Studios
When: 1968-74

**THE BEATLES** recorded *Hey Jude* and songs from *The White Album* here in autumn 1968. The studio piano, used on *Hey Jude*, was also used by Elton John on *Goodbye Yellow Brick Road*, and by Queen on *Bohemian Rhapsody*.

The Beatles used this studio, rather than the usual Abbey Road Studio No.2, because it was equipped with a new eight-track recording system. Abbey Road was still a four-track.

Lennon wrote for *The White Album* using material from many sources. Once George Martin gave him a magazine on guns with the headline *Happiness Is A Warm Gun*: "I read it. I thought it was a fantastic, insane thing to say, a warm gun means you just shot something."

Also...

**DAVID BOWIE** re-recorded *Space Oddity* at the studios on 20 June 1969, the day that he signed a record deal with Mercury.

*Space Oddity* became his first hit in both the UK and the US. Sales peaked at 130,000 in July when Neil Armstrong landed on the moon and the BBC used it when screening the event on television. This established Bowie's commercial success.

Years later he recorded a version of *The Prettiest Star* at Trident Studios, as a duet with Marc Bolan of T Rex. They were brought together by the producer, Tony Visconti, who worked with both men.

Also...

**GENESIS** recorded *Trespass,* their first Charisma LP, here in July 1970. The group had been offered a management contract and record deal by Tony Stratton-Smith, owner of Charisma Records, earlier in March 1970 and Genesis became the first group on the new label.  In September they recruited Phil Collins as drummer.

Also...

**SUPERTRAMP** recorded *Crime Of The Century*, their first hit album, at Trident during 1974. Produced by Ken Scott, it was considered to be of such a high production standard that audio-equipment manufacturers used it for testing their systems.

**17** | Where: 201 Wardour Street, The Vortex
What: **PUNK**
When: 1977

The Vortex took over as the place for punk-rock groups and their groupies to go after The Roxy, on Neal Street, had closed down.

**18** | Where: Corner Noel Street & Berwick Street
Who: **OASIS**
When: 1995

The cover photograph for *(What's The Story) Morning Glory* was taken on this Soho street corner. This was the group's second album and the best-selling album of 1995.

**19** | Where: 10A Poland Street, Anemone Studios
When: 1960s & 1970s

**ROD STEWART** recorded his first demo as a solo artist at these studios on 10 September 1964 after signing a record deal with Decca. The single *Good Morning Little Schoolgirl* was not a hit.

Also...

**THE JAM**'s first demo session was at these studios in February 1977. But it was disrupted by an IRA bomb explosion in Oxford Street. The following year, they released *A Bomb In Wardour Street*, as a B-side to *David Watts*.

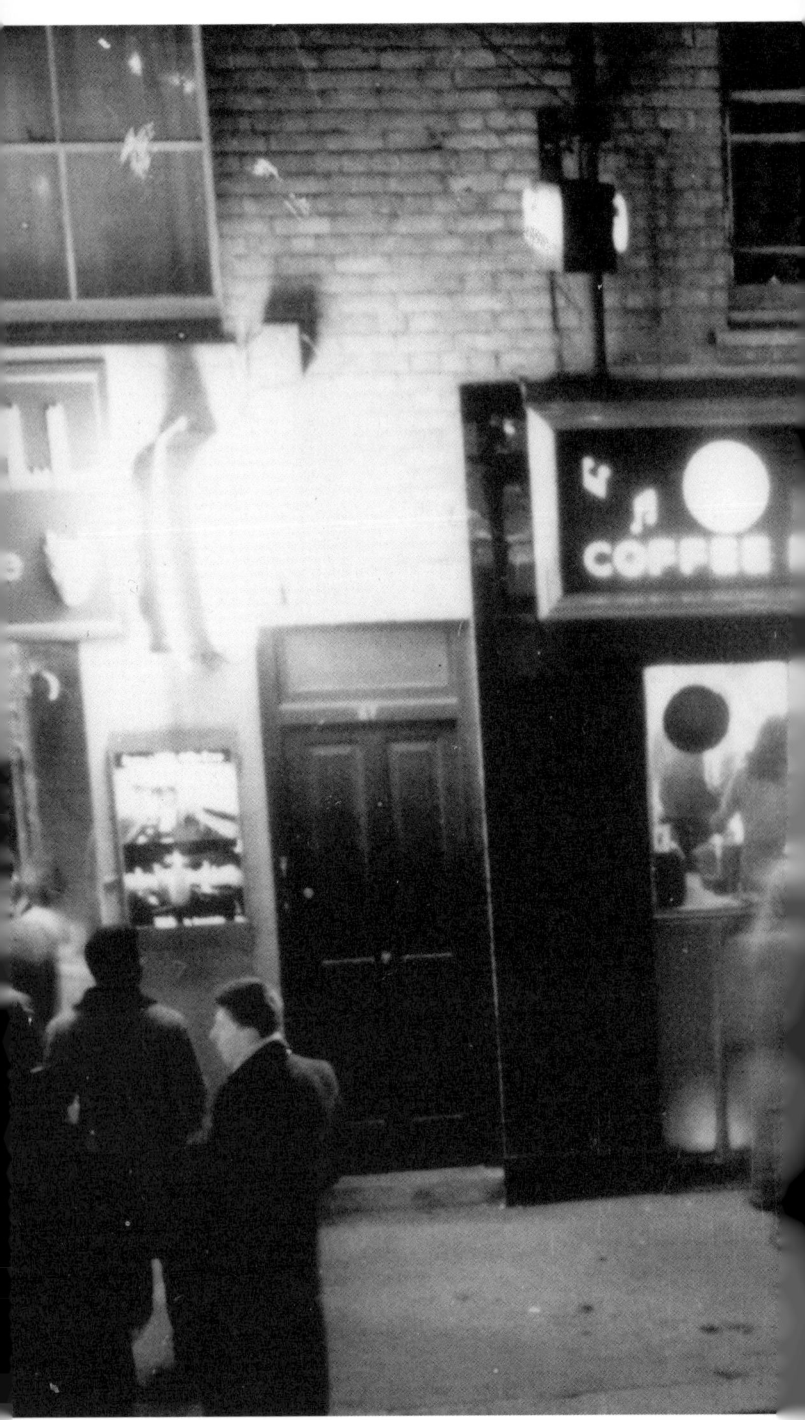


THE **2I'S COFFEE BAR** ON OLD COMPTON STREET

**20** | Where: Broadwick Street Public Toilets, the Gents
Who: **JOHN LENNON**
When: 27 November 1966

These public toilets, in the heart of Soho, were the location of John Lennon's part in the filming of an episode of 'Not Only But Also'.

The hit TV satirical show, headed by Peter Cook and Dudley Moore, required him to play the doorman of these toilets. The episode is famous for Lennon wearing his round 'grandfather' glasses in public, creating a new fashion.

**7 BROADWICK STREET** WHERE THE ROLLING STONES FORMED

**21** | Where: 7 Broadwick Street, Bricklayers Arms
Who: **THE ROLLING STONES**
When: March-April 1962

This is where The Rolling Stones first met, when guitarist Brian Jones had advertised auditions to join his blues band.

Bank clerk, Ian Stewart, was the first to turn up, impressing Jones with his piano playing. Next Mick Jagger and Keith Richards arrived, broke and dirty, also off-key in their performances. However their attitude fitted the band and they were in.

Subsequently, the group rehearsed at the pub three times a week.

The pub is now a jewellers.

**22** | Where: 59 Old Compton Street, the Dome Café
When: 1950s

Here in the 1950s was the 2i's Coffee Bar with a rock and roll club upstairs. It became a place where hopeful young performers auditioned:

**TOMMY STEELE** was discovered at the club in 1956 by Larry Parnes. Parnes changed the youngster's name from Hicks to Steele and so started his stable of rock and rollers, which soon included Marty Wilde and Billy Fury.

Steele, born at 52 Frean Street, Bermondsey, had left the Merchant Navy only two weeks before.

And...

**CLIFF RICHARD**'s career was also launched at the 2is in 1958.

And...

**THE SHADOWS'** Hank Marvin and Bruce Welch arrived in London in September 1958 from Newcastle. They were seen playing here and invited to join Cliff Richard's backing band, The Drifters. After changing their name to The Shadows in July 1959, they went on to become the most successful British instrumental group with five No.1 records, alongside seven with Cliff Richard.

And...

**MARC BOLAN** worked in the coffee bar in the early 1960s serving drinks. His parents had a stall in nearby Berwick Street market.

At around the same time, Peter Grant, later manager of Led Zeppelin, worked here as a bouncer.

**23** | Where: 57 Old Compton Street, Comptons of Soho
Who: **CLIFF RICHARD**
When: 1950s

Cliff Richard was known by his real name, Harry Webb, until his manager, John Foster, thought up the new one. It was whilst at this bar, then called the Swiss Pub, that the name was decided. The Swiss Pub was also a music venue and was the site of The Drifter's (later The Shadows) first gig.

**24** | Where: Corner Old Compton & Frith Streets
Who: **THE CLASH**
When: June 1976

Mick Jones met Joe Strummer on this street corner in Soho. They were both on their way to see a Tom Waits gig at Ronnie Scott's.

Mick Jones persuaded Joe Strummer to leave The 101ers (named after the squat he lived in at 101 Warburton Terrace in Walthamstow) and to join his new band, The Clash. Strummer, an ex-student of the Central School of Art and Design on Southampton Row, became the lead vocalist and guitarist of the new punk group.

The Clash rivalled The Sex Pistols as leaders of the punk movement.

**25** | Where: 47 Frith Street, Ronnie Scott's
When: Late 1960s onwards

**THE WHO** first played their rock opera *Tommy* to the media in May 1969. The opera, about *"the deaf, dumb, blind kid who sure plays a mean pinball"*, became an instant success.

Also...

**GENESIS** were signed up in March 1970 by Tony Stratton-Smith to Charisma Records, his own record label, after seeing them playing at Ronnie Scott's.

**Ronnie Scott's** on Frith Street

Peter Gabriel was the main creative force of the group in their early years. Living in flats at Boston Place, Marylebone and then Bramham Gardens, Earls Court, Gabriel developed his song-writing. It was when he lived at Bramham Gardens that he wrote *The Knife*, an early Genesis single on the LP, *Trespass*. And...

**JIMI HENDRIX** came to Ronnie Scott's on 16 September 1970, the night before he died. The Eric Burdon Band were playing at the club and Hendrix joined them for a jam session. It was his last performance.

**26** | Where: 1 Soho Square, MPL Communications
Who: **PAUL McCARTNEY**
When: 1970s onwards

The offices of Paul McCartney's music publishing company, which includes his own work, musicals and the entire Buddy Holly catalogue. In the basement is a recording studio which McCartney occasionally uses.

It was here that McCartney named his band, Wings, inspired by the birth of his daughter Stella at Kings College Hospital in Denmark Hill. The group started out playing small venues, whilst touring Britain in a van. Like The Beatles, McCartney wanted to build the group up slowly.

Despite great commercial success, McCartney has only occasionally received the critical acclaim he had with The Beatles, for example with *Band On The Run*

Indeed, McCartney has said: "I know I've lost my edge. I like edgy stuff actually. But I need a kind of outside injection, stimulation."

**27** | Where: 57 Dean Street, St Anne's Church
Who: **PAUL SIMON**
When: 1965

When Paul Simon was living in London in the mid 1960s, he sheltered from a rain storm in the church. Whilst in the church, he wrote *Blessed,* a song about religious hypocrisy.

**28** | Where: 69 Dean Street, Billy's Club
What: **NEW ROMANTICS**
When: 1980s

The New Romantic movement began at Billy's Club during the weekly Bowie Nights. Organised by Steve Strange, ex-Visage, and Rusty Egan, the club launched both Gary Numan and Spandau Ballet.

**29** | Where: 20 Old Compton Street, Pollo Bar & Restaurant
Who: **PINK FLOYD**
When: 1965

Syd Barrett always ate at this restaurant in the early days of Pink Floyd when he lived across the road in Earlham Street.

He played the Chinese games, I Ching and Go, at the restaurant, which inspired the song *Chapter 24* about change and success.

ʟ McCartney's **MPL Communications** on Soho Square

GEORGE MICHAEL OUTSIDE THE **ROYAL COURTS OF JUSTICE** DURING HIS CASE WITH SONY RECO

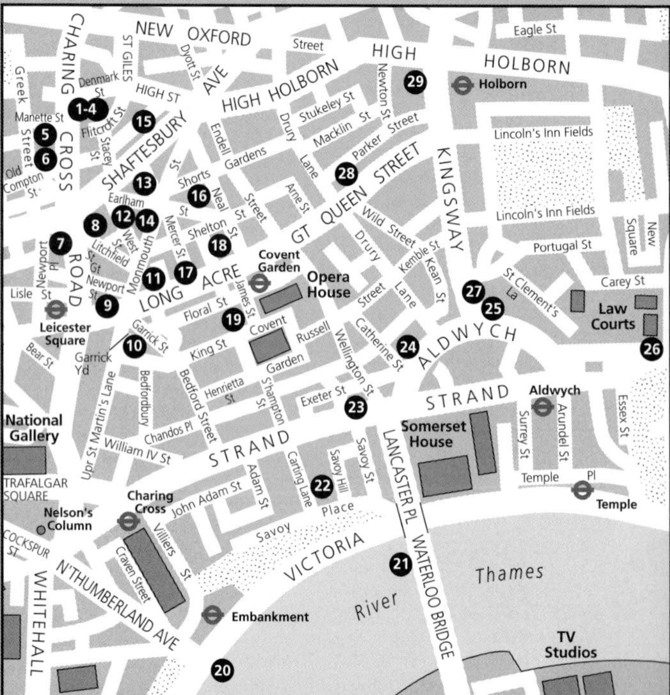

NEW OXFORD Street
HIGH HOLBORN
HOLBORN
Eagle St
Holborn
CHARING CROSS ROAD
ST GILES HIGH ST
Denmark St
Dyott St
Greek Street
Manette St
Old Compton St
Flitcroft St
Stacey St
SHAFTESBURY AVE
Endell St
Drury Lane
Stukeley St
Macklin St
Newton St
Parker Street
Shorts Gardens
Earlham St
Neal Street
Arne St
GT QUEEN STREET
KINGSWAY
Lincoln's Inn Fields
Mercer St
West St
Litchfield St
Monmouth St
Gt Newport St
Newport Pl
Shelton St
Wild Street
Kemble St
Kean St
Portugal St
New Square
Lisle St
Leicester Square
LONG ACRE
James St
Covent Garden
Opera House
Floral St
Drury Lane
St Clement's La
Carey St
Law Courts
Garrick St
Garrick Yd
Bear St
King St
Covent Garden
Russell St
Wellington St
Catherine St
ALDWYCH
Bedfordbury
Bedford Street
Henrietta St
S'hampton St
Exeter St
STRAND
Aldwych
Arundel St
Essex St
Surrey St
National Gallery
Upr St Martin's Lane
Chandos Pl
William IV St
Somerset House
LANCASTER PL
Temple Pl
Temple
TRAFALGAR SQUARE
Adam St
Carting Lane
Savoy Hill
Savoy St
John Adam St
Charing Cross
Nelson's Column
Savoy Place
Villiers St
COCKSPUR ST
Craven Street
VICTORIA
WATERLOO BRIDGE
Thames
River
WHITEHALL
N'THUMBERLAND AVE
Embankment
TV Studios
1-4
5
6
7
8
9
10
11
12
13
14
15
16
17
18
19
20
21
22
23
24
25
26
27
28
29

# Covent Garden WC2

**1** | Where: 6-8 Denmark Street
When: 1970s & 1980s

**BADFINGER's** Pete Ham and Tom Evans were signed to The Beatles' Apple label. After Paul McCartney had written their 1969 hit *Come And Get It*, they lived for a while at the flat, where they wrote *Without You*. Despite the song's massive success when recorded by Harry Nilsson, neither Ham nor Evans received fair compensation or recognition. This led to depression and both committed suicide: Ham in 1975 and Evans in 1983. Mariah Carey covered the song in 1996.
And…
**THE SEX PISTOLS** rehearsed and wrote their first hits, *Anarchy In The UK* and *Pretty Vacant*, in the warehouse in 1976. Glen Matlock, Steve Jones and Paul Cook lived in the flat on the first floor with no sanitation. Johnny Rotten joined them, but also lived in a squat in Hampstead.

The rent on the building was paid for by Malcolm McLaren, who sponsored The Sex Pistols and intended to use them as promotion for the outrageous bondage clothes sold at his shop, Sex, on the King's Road.
And…
**SIOUXSIE & THE BANSHEES** wrote their first song in the warehouse in 1977 called *Love In A Void*.
And…
**BANANARAMA** first sang together here in the early 1980s. They formed after playing in Paul Cook's group, The Professionals, and were initially the backing group to Fun Boy Three.

**2** | Where: 9A Denmark Street, La Gioconda
When: 1960s

The coffee shop was a regular meeting place for bands in the 1960s, as it was situated in the heart of the music industry that inhabited Denmark Street.
Amongst others…
**THE SMALL FACES** voted to turn professional here in October 1965, when, over a few bottles of beer, they decided to accept a deal offered by Decca.
And…
**DAVID BOWIE** was introduced to The Lower Third here in June 1966. The Lower Third was the last band that Bowie joined before starting his solo career.

**3** | Where: 20 Denmark Street, Mills Music Publishers
Who: **ELTON JOHN**
When: 1963

When Elton John left Pinner County Grammar School in 1963, he got a job in the warehouse of Mills Music Publishers. He worked here for eighteen months as a boy and general help: "I landed myself a job as a junior in Mills Music … It was what I wanted. I was bored with school and happy to leave, though my music teacher protested at my decision."
By night he played in his band, Bluesology.

**4** | Where: 4 Denmark Street, Regent Sound Studios
When: 1960s

**THE ROLLING STONES** recorded the Buddy Holly song, *Not Fade Away*, at these studios on 10 January 1964. This became their first top three hit in the UK. To distinguish them from The Beatles, The Stones developed a very aggressive sound.

Also...

**THE KINKS'** first recording session was also in January 1964 at Regent Sound. They recorded *Its Alright*, *One Fine Day* and *I Believed You*. All were produced by Shel Talmy, the American record producer for The Who. These demos secured the band a recording contract with Pye Records.

And...

**GENESIS** recorded their first single *Silent Sun* here in late 1967.

At this time Peter Gabriel, Mike Rutherford, Tony Banks, Chris Stewart and Tony Phillips were still at Charterhouse school. They had sent a demo tape to an ex-pupil of their school, the impresario Jonathan King. Impressed by the tape, King took on the management of the band. He changed their name to Genesis from The Anon and financed this first recording session.

THE SEX PISTOLS PLAYING AN EARLY GIG

**5** | Where: 109 Charing Cross Road, St Martin's School Of Art
When: 1970s

**THE SEX PISTOLS** played their first gig here on 6 November 1975. The college was a meeting place for early punk groups.

During this gig, Johnny Rotten's friend, Sid Vicious, began to jump up and down, with his feet close together and his hands by his side. Others copied and this became punk's contribution to dance, the 'pogo'.

And...

**PULP**'s Jarvis Cocker studied film-making at St Martin's after turning down a place at Oxford University. Pulp was formed in his hometown Sheffield when he was 16 and they moved down to London with Cocker.

**6** | Where: 111 Charing Cross Road, The Marquee Club
When: 1990s

This is the present location of The Marquee Club, which remains an important venue for launching groups.

**7** | Where: 77 Charing Cross Road, Dobell's Music Shop
Who: **BOB DYLAN**
When: January 1963

On one of his first trips to the UK, Bob Dylan recorded under the name 'Blind Boy Grunt' on an album by folk singer Richard Farina. This became his first recording in England, taking place in the basement of this shop.

**8** | Where: 27 Litchfield Street, Bunjies Folk Club
Who: **PAUL SIMON**
When: Early 1960s

Paul Simon used to play here, along with Al Stewart, the Scottish folk singer.

Simon had left law school in New York to come to Europe, firstly Paris, then London.

In London, Simon lived with friend, Judith Piepe, in Cable Street, East London, where Stewart also stayed occasionally.

Piepe discovered Simon playing at another folk club, The Flamingo. She helped to promote his music in the UK through her work as a radio producer.

He wrote many of his early songs whilst living in Cable Street. One was *Kathy's Song*, inspired by a girl he had met at his first UK concert at the Railway Inn, in Brentwood, Essex.

**9** | Where: 10-11 Great Newport Street, Studio 51
When: 10 September 1963

Studio 51 was a jazz club of the 1960s, where The Stones once rehearsed and had a daytime slot.

**THE ROLLING STONES** were looking for a follow-up single to their first hit *Come On*. Despite going through all the songs they knew, nothing seemed appropriate and they were growing desperate.

However on 10 September 1963, their manager Andrew Oldham bumped into ohn Lennon and Paul McCartney in nearby Jermyn Street. McCartney and ennon were returning from a Variety Club Award lunch at the Savoy.

Oldham had done some publicity for The Beatles and asked them to help him out. They agreed and went to the club.

There, Lennon and McCartney told The Stones they had a song that might do. ut it only had one verse. They would need five minutes to finish it. To The tones' amazement, the pair sat down and completed the song: *I Wanna Be Your Man* was the result. Within weeks, The Stones released their version of *I Wanna Be Your Man* and had a second hit.

Jagger and Richards were inspired by the simplicity and speed of the omposition to write their own songs. When told by Oldham of the increased icome for songwriters, the pair soon went to work.

lso...

**HE YARDBIRDS**, with new member Eric Clapton, used to improvise at the club hen they took over from The Rolling Stones as the resident band.

**10** | Where: Garrick Yard, St Martin's Lane, The Little Theatre
Who: **DAVID BOWIE**
When: August 1967

Bowie learnt dance and mime here with Lindsay Kemp. Mime played a large part in Bowie's stage performance in later years.

**11** | Where: Upper St Martin's Lane, Slug & Lettuce
Who: **KEITH MOON-THE WHO**
When: 7 September 1978

This was the location for the 1978 Buddy Holly Convention party, organised by Paul McCartney. Keith Moon spent his last night at the party here before dying at his girlfriend's flat in Curzon Place.

**12** | Where: 2 Earlham Street
Who: **SYD BARRETT-PINK FLOYD**
When: Late 1965

Whilst living here, Syd Barrett wrote much of his material for the first two Pink Floyd albums and his solo albums.

And here he named the band, The Pink Floyd Sound after two blues men from Georgia, USA: Pink Anderson and Floyd Council. For some time the group were called The Pink Floyd before 'The' was dropped.

Pink Floyd played their first gig at the Countdown Club in Queen's Gate in South Kensington.

**13** | Where: Cnr Earlham Street & Shaftesbury Avenue, Moonies Bar
Who: **THE SEX PISTOLS**
When: 1976

In the early days of The Sex Pistols, Glen Matlock was drinking away his dole cheque in this bar. He wrote *Pretty Vacant* whilst listening to Abba's *SOS* over the sound system.

After Johnny Rotten added the lyrics, the demo was recorded at Majestic Studios, 146 Clapham High Street. Unfortunately, by the time *Pretty Vacant* became a hit, Matlock had left the group.

**14** | Where: 28 Earlham Street, Flats 14-15 Fielding Court
Who: **DAVE STEWART**
When: 1990s

Dave Stewart bought these two flats after leaving The Eurythmics.
And...
**BLUR**'s Alex James lives around the corner in a converted Georgian cheese factory off Seven Dials.

**15** | Where: 135-139 Shaftesbury Avenue, Saville Theatre
Who: **BRIAN EPSTEIN-THE BEATLES**
When: 1960s

The Beatles' manager, Brian Epstein, owned the theatre and used it as a rock venue, for amongst others, Jimi Hendrix.

Epstein, a frustrated actor since his days at RADA, intended to use the theatre to launch his own acting career. But this never materialised.

**16** | Where: 41-43 Neal Street, The Roxy
What: **PUNK**
When: 1 January 1977-23 April 1977

This punk-rock club opened on 1 January 1977 for just over three months. **THE PRETENDERS**' Chrissie Hynde played her live UK debut with the Johnny Moped Band at the first night of the club, headlined by The Clash.
And…
**ADAM & THE ANTS** performed for the first time at the closing-night party of the club. Also playing were Siouxsie and The Banshees with their guitarist Marco Pirroni. The two got on and Pirroni later joined Adam Ant, real name Stewart Goddard, as song-writing partner.

**17** | Where: 28 Long Acre, New Musical Express
Who: **THE PRETENDERS**
When: 1 January 1974

Chrissie Hynde spent a short time as a journalist on the music newspaper when she first came to London. Arriving from America, she met journalist, Nick Kent, who had connections with the punk movement. It was he who asked her to write for the paper. She wrote the occasional review, her first was of a Neil Diamond album.

**18** | Where: 5 Langley Street, Eddie Ryan Drum Renovations
Who: **THE PRETENDERS**
When: 1978

The Pretenders rehearsed here in 1978. Chrissie Hynde had just assembled the band: Pete Farndon, James Honeyman-Scott and Gerry Mackleduff, who was replaced by Martin Chambers later in the year. They recorded The Kinks' song *Stop Your Sobbing*, which was released the following year.

In 1980, Hynde began a three-year relationship with Ray Davies, of The Kinks, and they had a daughter.

**19** | Where: Covent Garden Piazza, The Rock Garden
Who: **THE SMITHS**
When: 23 March 1983

This is where the group played their London debut. The success of the gig led to their signing to Rough Trade Records in London, rather than to Factory Records of their home-town Manchester.

**20** | Where: Victoria Embankment, Charing Cross Pier
Who: **THE SEX PISTOLS**
When: 7 June 1977

The Sex Pistols' new record company, Virgin Records, chartered a boat on the Thames on the day of the Silver Jubilee celebrations. Outside the Houses of Parliament, the group sang *Anarchy In The UK*. They were arrested when they returned to shore.

This was filmed for 'The Great Rock 'N' Roll Swindle' by Julian Temple, who later directed 'Absolute Beginners' with Patsy Kensit and David Bowie.

**21** | Where: Waterloo Bridge
Who: **THE KINKS**
When: June 1967

As a child, Ray Davies had his tonsils out at St Thomas' Hospital on the banks of the Thames. Later as a teenager, he crossed Waterloo Bridge daily on his way to art college in Croydon.

His past memories, mixed with the present, inspired *Waterloo Sunset*.

The song's two lovers, Terry and Julie, were named after the stars of 'Far from the Madding Crowd', Terence Stamp and Julie Christie.

*Waterloo Sunset* was the last record produced by Shel Talmy. After that, Ray Davies produced all the Kinks' records.

BOB DYLAN WITH JOAN BAEZ OUTSIDE THE **SAVOY HOTEL** IN 1965

**22** | Where: Savoy Place, Savoy Hotel
When: 1960s-1980s

**BOB DYLAN** based himself here during his early tour to Britain in April 1965.

He used the road behind the hotel for the promotional film of *Subterranean Homesick Blues*. The hand-held captions, with instructions like 'Think', were written in his suite the night before with Donovan.

On a subsequent tour to England, he filmed 'Don't Look Back', set in Denmark Street and other London locations.

Dylan was at the height of his creative powers in 1965 and was seen as the greatest poet by his contemporaries. The leading British stars came to the hotel room to pay their respects. Guests included The Beatles and The Stones.

After his meeting, John Lennon said:

"I started thinking about my own emotions. I would just try to express what I thought about myself. I think it was Dylan that helped me realise that by hearing his work."

Later, however, Lennon said:

"In those days I was writing obscurely like Dylan, never saying what you mean but giving the impression of something, where more or less can be read into it. Its a good game ... Dylan got away with murder. I thought, well, I can write this crap too. You know, you just stick a few images together and you call it poetry."

Marianne Faithfull said that Dylan tried to seduce her by writing pages of poetry which he handed to her, one at time, as they were completed.

Also...

**MICK JAGGER** stayed in Suite 312 of the Savoy in November 1983, promoting The Stones' album, *Undercover*.

**23** | Where: Wellington Street, London Lyceum
When: 1960s-1980s

**JOHN LENNON** played his last live gig in England here on 15 December 1969. He played a UNICEF 'Peace for Christmas' benefit with The Plastic Ono Band.

Also...

**BOB MARLEY** recorded the breakthrough reggae album, *Live!*, at a concert here on 18 July 1975.

Also...

**U2** exchanged contracts with Island Records in March 1980 in the female toilets of this concert venue. Their first major record deal was for four albums. Each member of the group is now worth about £75 million.

**24** | Where: 11 Aldwych
Who: **IVOR NOVELLO**
When: 1914-1951

vor Novello lived in a top floor flat from 1914 to his death in 1951. He wrote many popular songs and is remembered by the Ivor Novello Award given annually to popular songwriters. Recipients of the award have included Gary Glitter, Elton John and George Michael.

**25** | Where: Houghton Street, London School Of Economics
Who: **MICK JAGGER-THE ROLLING STONES**
When: Early 1960s

Mick Jagger attended the LSE after leaving school in Dartford. It was at Dartford train station on his way to a lecture here that he re-met Keith Richard.

**26** | Where: Strand, Royal Courts Of Justice
When: 1960s-1990s

Most major stars have at some point had recourse to the law.

**THE OZ** obscenity trial was held here in January 1967. Oz was the most influential underground magazine of the 1960s and was established by Australian Richard Neville at 70 Clarendon Road, Holland Park. It gave early exposure to Germaine Greer, Barry Humphries and Clive James.

Oz was prosecuted over its 'School Kids' issue. A fund was set up, with John Lennon and Yoko Ono writing and recording a song in support of the magazine. Also...

**THE BEATLES** officially ended here in March 1971 when Paul McCartney disbanded the group because of his disagreement over manager Allen Klein's financial control. A receiver was appointed by the court to administer their affairs.

Also...

**FRANKIE GOES TO HOLLYWOOD**'s lead singer, Holly Johnson won a case against ZTT Records and Perfect Songs in the High Court on 10 February 1988. The court reversed the company's injunction on his solo record contract with EMI. Johnson was one of the very few pop stars to win in a contract case with a record company.

And in the 1990s...

**JASON DONOVAN** sued 'The Face' magazine after being accused of homosexuality. He won half a million pounds in damages.

And...

**GEORGE MICHAEL** failed to break his contract with Sony. He lost half a million pounds in the court costs of the failed attempt. He has since left Sony.

**27** | Where: 4-12 Kingsway, TV House, Rediffusion Studios
When: Early 1960s

'Ready Steady Go' was a pioneering TV pop programme that launched new groups in the early 1960s. It was filmed here every Friday evening.

Also...

**ROD STEWART** met Ron Wood, a session bass-player, at the studios after recording the show on 6 August 1964. Rod Stewart was making his TV debut.

In 1969, Wood introduced Stewart to The Small Faces, whilst they were rehearsing at The Rolling Stones' studios in Bermondsey after Steve Marriott had left. They needed a new singer but took a lot of persuading as Stewart was thought self-centred and unsuitable.

**28** | Where: 4 Great Queen Street, Blitz Club
Who: **SPANDAU BALLET**
When: 6 February 1979

Influential New Romantic club.

Spandau Ballet made their live public debut at the club's Christmas Party in December 1979. Though offered a contract with Island Records, they turned it down in favour of setting up their own label.

**29** | Where: 129 Kingsway, De Lane Lea Studios
When: 1960s

**THE ROLLING STONES** recorded *I Wanna Be Your Man*, the song written by Lennon and McCartney, here on 7 October 1963 in a day-long session. The Stones had been given the song at Studio 51 by John Lennon and Paul McCartney, a couple of weeks before.

*I Wanna Be Your Man* made No.12 in the UK charts, enabling them to appear on the first ever Top Of The Pops, which was also their first TV appearance. Soon after they played their first headline concert at the Granada Cinema in Harrow.

And...

**THE ANIMALS** recorded *The House Of The Rising Sun* here on 30 May 1964, the day they finished a tour with Chuck Berry.

They arrived in London at 7.45 for the 8.00 am start. Their producer Mickie Most did not like the song and had only booked a half hour session, allowing them only one take.

A traditional song adapted by the group, *The House Of The Rising Sun* became their biggest hit.

And...

**THE JIMI HENDRIX EXPERIENCE** recorded for the first time together on 23 October 1966 at these studios. Their manager, Chas Chandler, who had been in The Animals, was able to get a special rate. Amongst the first songs recorded were *Hey Joe* and *Stonefree*.

The Jimi Hendrix Experience consisted of Hendrix, Mitch Mitchell and Noel Redding.

The Sex Pistols signing to A&M Records outside **Buckingham Palace** in 1977

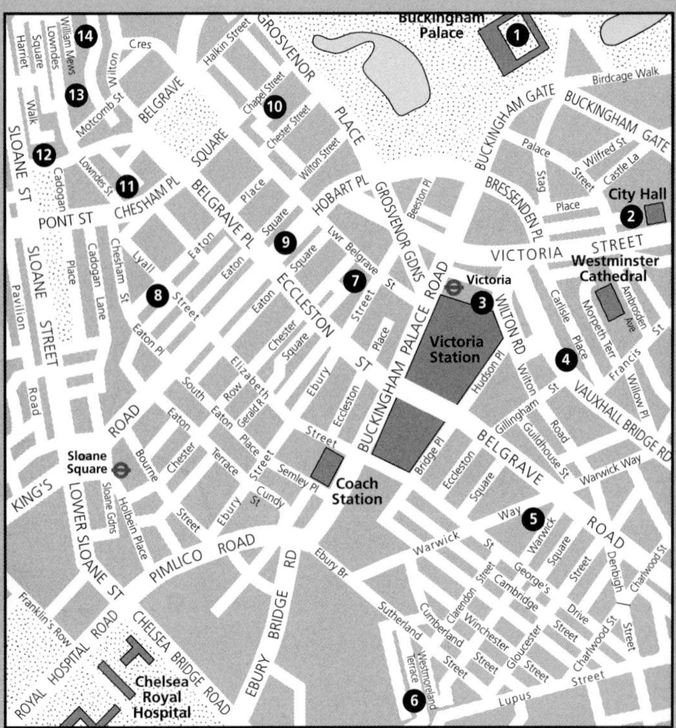

Buckingham Palace
1
Birdcage Walk
BUCKINGHAM GATE
BUCKINGHAM GATE
Palace Street
Wilfred St
Castle La
City Hall
2
Stag Place
BRESSENDEN PL
Beeston Pl
VICTORIA STREET
Westminster Cathedral
Ambrosden Ave
Francis St
Morpeth Terr
Carlisle Place
Willow Pl
4
VAUXHALL BRIDGE RD
Victoria
3
Victoria Station
WILTON RD
Hudson Pl
Wilton Road
Gillingham St
Guildhouse St
Warwick Way
BELGRAVE ROAD
Eccleston Square
Bridge Pl
BUCKINGHAM PALACE ROAD
GROSVENOR GDNS
GROSVENOR PLACE
HOBART PL
Wilton Street
Chester Street
Chapel Street
10
Halkin Street
BELGRAVE SQUARE
Wilton Cres
14
William Mews
Lowndes Square
Harriet Walk
13
Motcomb St
12
SLOANE ST
Cadogan Place
Lowndes St
11
CHESHAM PL
PONT ST
BELGRAVE PL
Eaton Place
9
Eaton Square
Lwr Belgrave St
7
Eccleston Street
Eccleston Place
ECCLESTON ST
Lyall Street
8
Chesham St
Cadogan Lane
SLOANE STREET
Pavilion Road
Eaton Pl
Eaton Square
Chester Square
Elizabeth Street
South Eaton Place
Eaton Row
Gerald R
Ebury Street
Eccleston Street
Semley Pl
Coach Station
Cundy St
Ebury St
Chester Row
Eaton Terrace
Bourne Street
KING'S ROAD
Sloane Square
Sloane Gdns
Holbein Place
LOWER SLOANE ST
PIMLICO ROAD
EBURY BRIDGE RD
Ebury Br
Warwick Way
5
Warwick Square
St George's Drive
Cambridge Street
Denbigh Street
Charlwood St
Clarendon Street
Sutherland Terrace
Cumberland Street
Winchester Street
Gloucester Street
Charlwood St
Lupus Street
Westmoreland Terrace
6
Franklin's Row
ROYAL HOSPITAL ROAD
CHELSEA BRIDGE ROAD
Chelsea Royal Hospital

# Victoria & Belgravia SW1

**1** | Where: Buckingham Palace
When: 1960s & 1970s

**THE BEATLES** were made Members of the British Empire by the Queen on 26 October 1965.

John Lennon later returned his in protest of Britain's support of the US in the war in South East Asia.

In 1997 Paul McCartney was knighted here.

Also…

**THE SEX PISTOLS** signed to A&M records on 10 March 1977 in front of Buckingham Palace, soon releasing their single *God Save The Queen* to coincide with the Jubilee celebrations.

Despite being banned, the record reached No.1 in the UK charts, though manipulation by the BBC placed it at No.2.

Six days later, A&M cancelled the contract and Virgin Records took over. But The Pistols kept the £75,000 advance from A&M.

**2** | Where: Victoria Street, Caxton Hall
When: 1970s onwards

**RINGO STARR** married Maureen Cox, his first wife, at Westminster's registry office on 11 February 1965.

And…

**ADAM FAITH** married Jackie Irving, an ex-girlfriend of Cliff Richard, on 19 August 1967.

**3** | Where: Victoria Station, Platform 8
Who: **DAVID BOWIE**
When: 3 May 1976

Site of David Bowie's infamous Nazi salute.

He was passing through England en-route to Berlin. Though Bowie claimed he was simply waving to the crowd, the month before he had been stopped at the border of Russia and Poland with Nazi books. It was a disturbed time for Bowie, after several years of drug dependency in Los Angeles. Much of this was reflected in the music he wrote whilst living in Berlin, *Heroes* and *Low*.

**4** | Where: 306 Vauxhall Bridge Road, Axfords
Who: **IAN DURY**
When: February 1978

Ian Dury was photographed outside this shop with his son for the cover of *New Boots And Panties*. Dury used Axfords as the location for the cover, as he frequently visited the shop whilst living in Vauxhall. The LP stayed in the charts for over 90 weeks.

5 | Where: 79a Warwick Square
Who: **DAVID BOWIE**
When: Late 1965

Home of Ralph Horton, Bowie's first manager and also of The Moody Blues.

It was Horton who changed his name from David Jones to David Bowie. Bowie lived here for several months and wrote some of his early songs.

6 | Where: 22 Westmoreland Terrace
Who: **THE SMALL FACES**
When: 26 December 1965-1966

Manager Don Arden rented this house for The Small Faces. Though keeping them on a small wage, Arden continually pressured the group into making more hit songs. Vocalist Steve Marriott actually collapsed on the TV show, 'Ready Steady Go', in June 1966.

They took it in turns to write songs, often in the upstairs toilet, as it was the only place with peace and quiet. The first single they wrote, *Hey Girl*, came out in May 1966, followed later in the year by *All Or Nothing*. Both were written by guitarist Ronnie Lane and Marriott.

The house was also a popular hang-out for others in the music business. The Beatles' manager Brian Epstein had his first LSD trip here, as Ian McLagan, the group's organist, remembers:

> "It was a madhouse. Me, Ronnie and Steve lived there for a year. We'd get back from a gig, score some hash and just go. It was the party: people used to come round just to watch us. We had all the best acid and all the best fun. Brian Epstein had his first trip there."

THE SMALL FACES OUTSIDE **22 WESTMORELAND TERRACE**

HOMES OF THE WHO'S PETE TOWNSHEND:
**20 EBURY STREET** ... ... AND **84 EATON PLACE**

**7** | Where: 20 Ebury Street
Who: **PETE TOWNSHEND-THE WHO**
When: 1967-1968

Pete Townshend lived on the top floors of the house, which he soundproofed to use as a studio.

Here, he experimented with opera and wrote much of *Tommy*. Also at this time he discovered the teachings of the Indian guru, Meher Baba, which affected his work on *Tommy* and his later life.

**8** | Where: 84 Eaton Place
Who: **THE WHO**
When: 1960s

The Who's early managers, Kit Lambert and Chris Stamp, and their company, New Action, had their offices at No.84. Pete Townshend lived over the office with Lambert for a couple of months in 1964. Lambert encouraged Townshend to begin writing and it was here that *My Generation* was written.

**9** | Where: 65 Eaton Square
Who: **THE BEE GEES-BARRY GIBB**
When: 1968

Barry Gibb rented a basement flat here, soon after the group's first hit *Massachusetts*.

**10** | Where: 24 Chapel Street
Who: **BRIAN EPSTEIN-THE BEATLES**
When: Mid 1960s

London home of Beatles' manager, Brian Epstein.

The house was used for The Beatles' many business interests. One day Paul McCartney might decide on a film offer; another day John Lennon would choose a publisher for his books.

**24 Chapel Street** home of the Beatles' manager Brian Epstein

On 19 May 1967, the launch party for *Sergeant Pepper* was held here and Paul McCartney had his first date with Linda Eastman after their brief meeting at the Bag O'Nails club a few days before.

During the 1967 August bank holiday, Epstein took an overdose of pills and died at the house. Epstein had felt increasingly unneeded and depressed after the group had ceased touring to concentrate on studio work.

Devastated, The Beatles returned to London from a weekend in Wales with Maharishi Mahesh Yogi. After Epstein's death, they functioned less and less as a cohesive group and finally split in 1970.

**11** | Where: 8 Chesham Place
Who: **PETE TOWNSHEND- THE WHO**
When: Mid 1965

Pete Townshend lived here for most of 1965. A Union Jack flag hung on the walls, which he adopted as the group's emblem.

**8 Chesham Place** another Belgravia home of Pete Townshend

**12** | Where: Cadogan Place, Hyatt Carlton Tower Hotel
Who: **MADONNA**
When: 1990s

The hotel is used by Madonna when in London. Scenes from her 1991 film 'In Bed With Madonna' were shot here. On her most recent visit to London for the opening of 'Evita', she stayed at 55 Campden Hill Road W8, in a house owned by Lady Hindlip.

**23 Lowndes Square**

**13** | Where: 23 Lowndes Square
Who: **THE ROLLING STONES**
When: 1968

In the basement of this house, the interior shots for the film 'Performance' took place. Mick Jagger starred with Edward Fox and Keith Richards' girlfriend, Anita Pallenburg.

Jagger had an affair with Pallenburg during filming. This caused turmoil for Richards who waited outside in his Bentley composing songs and writing notes to Pallenburg and Jagger. Much of the *Let It Bleed* material comes from this time, in particular *You've Got The Silver*, his love song to Pallenburg, and *Gimme Shelter.*

The exterior shots of Performance were filmed in Powis Square, Notting Hill Gate.

**14** | Where: William Mews, Flat 7, 15 Whaddon House (private road)
Who: **THE BEATLES**
When: 1963-April 1964

George Harrison and Ringo Starr lived in a flat below their manager, Brian Epstein. He later suggested that the group move out of London to the Weybridge area to form a 'Beatle village'. Lennon and Starr moved to Weybridge and Harrison moved to nearby Esher. However McCartney preferred to stay in London.

Today, Ringo Starr is the only Beatle to maintain a regular London home: he owns a penthouse flat at the top of Whitelands House on the King's Road by Cheltenham Terrace. The £2.5 million apartment has a roof garden and panoramic views over London.

THE ROYAL ALBERT HALL

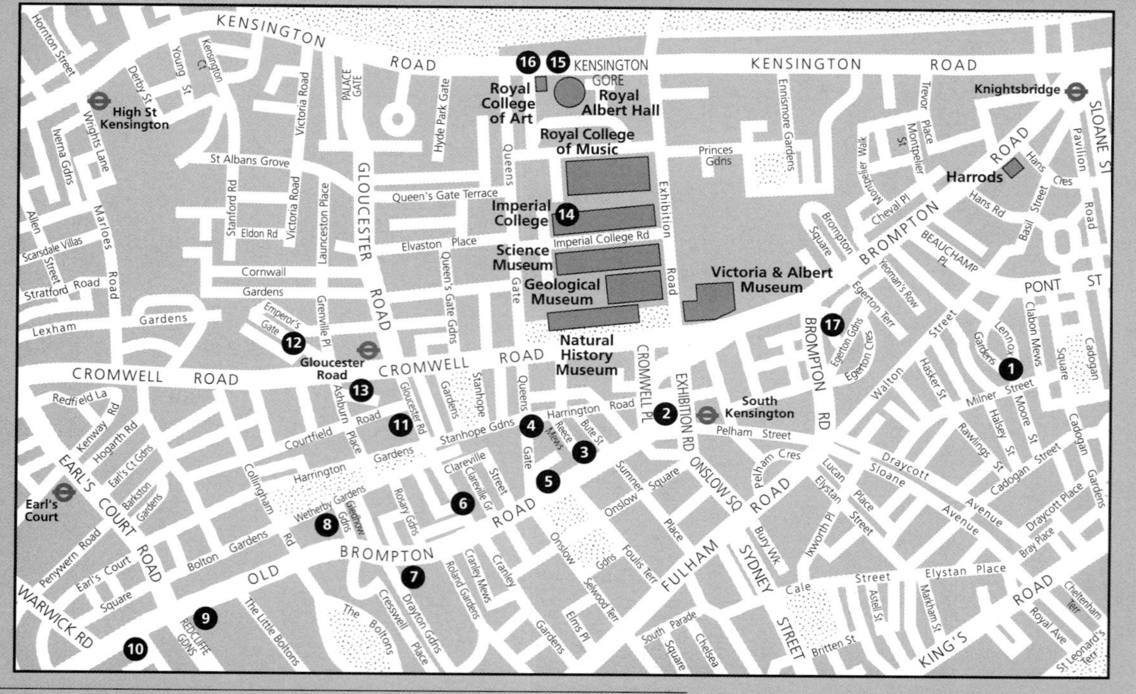


# Central London South Kensington SW1|5|7|10

# South Kensington SW1|5|7|10



1| Where: 29 Lennox Gardens
Who: **MARIANNE FAITHFULL**
When: 1965

Marianne Faithfull lived in the top floor flat during her late teens with her husband, the gallery owner John Dunbar, and their son.

Her first hit was in 1964 with *As Tears Go By*. It was written by Mick Jagger and Keith Richards, after Faithfull was spotted by their manager, Andrew Oldham: "I saw an angel with big tits and signed her".

2| Where: 4 Old Brompton Road, Egerton Court
Who: **SYD BARRETT-PINK FLOYD**
When: April 1968

Home of Storm Thorgersen, when he designed album covers for Pink Floyd.

Syd Barrett stayed at his flat in April 1968, after leaving the group. His increased drug dependency and erratic behaviour had caused the split. Dave Gilmour replaced him, but the group's managers resigned, believing Pink Floyd could not survive without Barrett.

**Egerton Court**

3| Where: Reece Mews
Who: **ROD STEWART**
When: Early 1964

Rod Stewart lived here with **John Baldry** when in his band, The Hoochie Coochie Men.

They had met at Twickenham train station when Baldry heard Stewart playing his harmonica. Baldry invited him to play at The Marquee Club the following week. The unemployed Stewart was given £35 and a job.

4| Where: 121 Queen's Gate, Blaises (demolished)
Who: **JIMI HENDRIX**
When: October 1966

Jimi Hendrix played his first London gig here, with Mitch Mitchell and Noel Redding, calling themselves The Experience.

5| Where: 109 Queen's Gate, Gore Hotel
Who: **THE ROLLING STONES**
When: 5 December 1968

In the hotel's 'Elizabethan' rooms, The Stones held a promotional party for *Beggars Banquet*.

Decca delayed the release of the album, refusing to allow The Stones' choice of cover: a graffiti covered lavatory wall. When a compromise was eventually found, the group were bored and angry by the obstinacy of their record company. They took pleasure in causing havoc at the party and threw cake and drink at the executives.

**6** | Where: 22 Clareville Grove
Who: **DAVID BOWIE**
When: August 1967-1968

David Bowie lived in the attic bedsit with girlfriend, Hermione Farthingale.

He met her in mid-1967 whilst studying mime in Floral Street, Covent Garden and they formed a short-lasting group called Feathers.

Bowie wrote *Space Oddity* at the flat and Farthingale inspired *"the girl with the mousy hair"* in *Life on Mars*.

**7** | Where: Drayton Gardens
Who: **YES**
When: Late 1968

Jon Anderson, Chris Squire, Tony Kaye, Bill Bruford and Peter Banks lived in a crumbling house after forming Yes. Music for *The Yes Album* was written here.

Soon the group was playing regularly at The Marquee club and had signed with Atlantic Records.

They released *Tales From Topographic Oceans* in 1973, which gave them their first gold disc. They had rehearsed for the album at Manticore Studios on North End Road.

**8** | Where: 10 Gledhow Gardens, Flat 1
Who: **ANDREW LLOYD WEBBER**
When: 1964

Andrew Lloyd Webber lived here in 1964 whilst writing *Jesus Christ Superstar*.

At the same time he wrote the initial music for *Joseph And The Amazing Technicolor Dreamcoat*.

Lloyd Webber was brought up in South Kensington: his childhood home Harrington Court no longer exists. He went to Westminster School before winning a scholarship to Oxford University.

After achieving success he bought further homes in the area at 11 West Eaton Place, 51 Eaton Place, and 37 Brompton Square.

Lloyd Webber is worth £600 million and he is the most financially successful composer in history. *Cats* has grossed over £1 billion, twice as much as Stephen Spielberg's film *'ET'*. Lloyd Webber has at least six shows on at the West End.

**9** | Where: Cnr Redcliffe Gardens & Old Brompton Road
Who: **THE BEATLES**
When: 18 December 1966

John Lennon wrote *A Day In The Life* after reading the newspaper account of a car-crash at these traffic lights.

His friend, Tara Browne, was killed instantly, whilst driving his Lotus Élan on LSD: *" I read the news today, about a lucky man who made the grade. He blew his mind out in a car. He didn't know that the lights had changed."*

Another Beatles' song inspired by a newspaper story was Paul McCartney's *She's Leaving Home*. The story of Melanie Cole, a teenager who ran away from home, in Amhurst Park, Stamford Hill, North London, hit the papers in 1967.

**The Troubadour Coffee Shop**

**10** | Where: 265 Old Brompton Road, The Troubadour
When: Early 1960s

Famous coffee bar for musicians.

**BOB DYLAN** performed here on his first trip to England. At the time he was still playing small venues. It was not until his second UK trip, to promote the albums *Freewheelin' Dylan* and *The Times They Are A Changing*, that he played to larger audiences: his first formal UK gig was at the Royal Festival Hall in May 1964.

Also…

**THE ROLLING STONES**' Charlie Watts met Alexis Korner here and was invited to play drums for Korner's band Blues Incorporated at The Marquee and The Ealing Club. Through Blues Incorporated he met the rest of The Rolling Stones.

Watts was born in Islington and went to Harrow Art College to study Graphic Design. He worked for advertising company, Hobson Charles & Grey, in Conduit Street and continued working there for the first few months after joining The Stones.

After living in Sussex for many years, Watts has moved to Halsdon House, Dalton, near Winkworth, in Devon. He is worth £40 million.

**11** | Where: 1 Courtfield Road
Who: **BRIAN JONES-THE ROLLING STONES**
When: 1966-68

rian Jones lived in a second floor flat in the building, overlooking the tube tation.

*Ruby Tuesday* was written here by Jones and Keith Richards. Mick Jagger later dded the lyrics.

Jones created much of The Stones' early flamboyant style with his then girlfriend Anita Pallenberg and the flat became a centre for the group and their friends.

He lived in several places in the area, including 29 Chester Square, Royal Avenue House on King's Road and 7 Elm Park Lane, Chelsea. His health was slowly deteriorating and he often checked into the Priory Hospital in Roehampton.

On 13 November 1968 he moved to Cotchford Farm in Hartfield, Sussex where A.A. Milne had written 'Winnie The Pooh'. Jones died there on 3 July 1969, less than a month after quitting the band. He was twenty-seven years old.

**12** | Where: 13 Emperors Gate (demolished)
Who: **JOHN LENNON**
When: 1964

John Lennon moved to his first home with his wife Cynthia and their son Julian in 1964.

The Lennons lived in the top maisonette, up six flights of stairs. Their balcony was overlooked by a student hostel opposite, from where fans took away what little privacy they thought they had.

Lennon wrote his first book, 'In His Own Right', here. He also had several affairs at the time, as he explained in describing the writing of his song, *Norwegian Wood*:

> "I was trying to write about an affair without telling my wife I was writing about an affair, so it was gobbledegook. I was sort of writing from my experiences, girls' flats, things like that."

**13** | Where: 101 Cromwell Road (demolished)
Who: **SYD BARRETT-PINK FLOYD**
When: 1968

Syd Barrett moved to a flat on this site, when he began the break with Pink Floyd. He spent his time here, experimenting with drugs and painting.

Barrett has inspired many musicians including David Bowie, and many songs including Pink Floyd's *Shine On You Crazy Diamond* and Donovan's lyrics from *Sunny South Kensington*: *"Come loon, soon down Cromwell Road, man, spread your wings"*.

**14** | Where: Prince Consort Road, Imperial College
Who: **BRIAN MAY & ROGER TAYLOR-QUEEN**
When: 1966-1969

Here, guitarist Brian May studied physics and astronomy and drummer Roger Taylor, biology.

Bass guitarist John Deacon went to nearby Chelsea College in Pulton Place, leaving with a first class degree in Electronics.

May moved to a house around the corner from the college on Queen's Gate Terrace after Queen's success in the late 1970s.

Today, May, Taylor and Deacon are each worth £38 million.

**15** | Where: Royal Albert Hall
When: 1960s-1990s

The Royal Albert Hall has been a leading Rock & Pop concert venue for over forty years. Many events have happened here:

**PAUL McCARTNEY** met his girlfriend Jane Asher at the Royal Albert Hall after playing a concert on 18 April 1963. Asher was sent to report for 'Radio Times' magazine, after her Juke Box Jury appearances had awarded her the title 'best known teenage girl'.

Also…

**JOHN LENNON & YOKO ONO** sat on the concert hall's stage in a black bag doing Bagism in 1968 as part of the Alchemical Wedding Christmas Party.

And…

**DEEP PURPLE** performed and recorded *Concerto For Group And Orchestra* here just after Roger Glover and Ian Gillan joined the group in September 1969. Composed by keyboardist Jon Lord, the *Concerto* was performed with the Royal Philharmonic Orchestra.

And…

**THE EVERLEY BROTHERS** chose the Albert Hall for their reunion on 23 September 1984.

And…

**ERIC CLAPTON** has played an annual set of concerts here at the beginning of most years since 1989. It was at the Albert Hall in November 1968 that Clapton played his last concert with Cream, splitting after less than two years together.

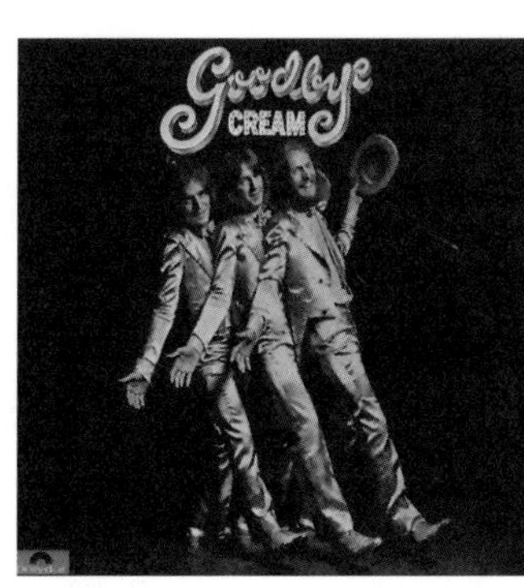


**16** | Where: Royal College Of Art
Who: **IAN DURY**
When: 1964-1966

After Walthamstow Art College, Ian Dury studied at the RCA. He then taught at Canterbury School of Art and formed the pub rock band, Kilburn and The High Roads.

At Walthamstow he was taught by Peter Blake who later designed the cover for The Beatles' *Sergeant Pepper's Lonely Hearts Club Band*.

**17** | Where: 28 Egerton Gardens, Franklin Hotel
When: 1990s

This small and private hotel is popular amongst visiting stars of Rock & Pop, including Sting and Tina Turner.

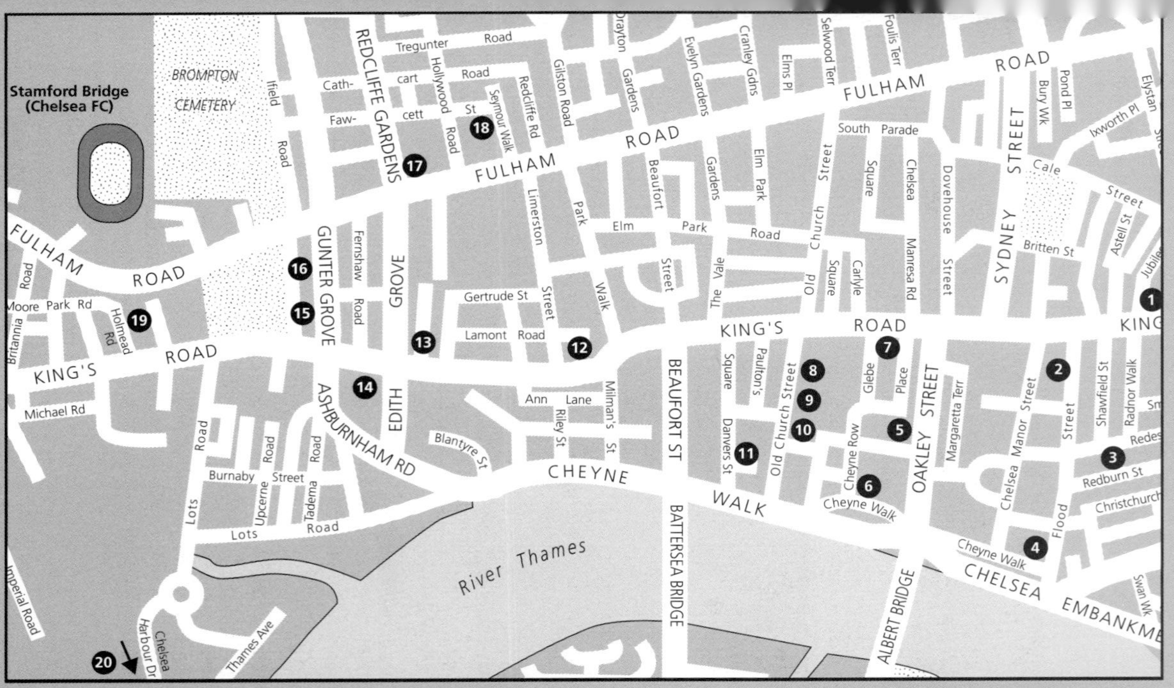
Stamford Bridge (Chelsea FC)
BROMPTON CEMETERY
FULHAM ROAD
KING'S ROAD
REDCLIFFE GARDENS
GUNTER GROVE
EDITH GROVE
ASHBURNHAM RD
CHEYNE WALK
BEAUFORT ST
BATTERSEA BRIDGE
OAKLEY STREET
ALBERT BRIDGE
SYDNEY STREET
CHELSEA EMBANKMENT
River Thames
Lots Road
Old Church Street
Cheyne Row
Glebe Place
Chelsea Manor Street
Flood Street
Imperial Road
Thames Ave
Chelsea Harbour Dr

# King's Road SW3|10

**1**| Where: 165 King's Road, the Pheasantry
Who: **ERIC CLAPTON**
When: November 1967

Eric Clapton shared a studio in the building with Australian artist Martin Sharp. Sharp was a founder of OZ magazine and designed the cover for the Cream album, *Disraeli Gears*.

Cream's *Sunshine Of Your Love* was written here, as was *Badge* by Clapton and George Harrison.

Clapton formed Cream with Ginger Baker and Jack Bruce in July 1966, securing a recording contract through Robert Stigwood. They played their first gig at Cooks Ferry Inn on the River Lea Towpath off Angel Road in north London. They were the first 'supergroup' before their split in November 1968.

THE PHEASANTRY

**2**| Where: 4 Chelsea Manor Studios, 1-11 Flood Street
Who: **THE BEATLES**
When: 30 March 1967

Site of the studio where The Beatles were photographed for the cover of *Sergeant Pepper*. The photograph was used with a collage by Peter Blake, who later designed the cover for *Do They Know It's Christmas?* the Band Aid single in 1984.

Blake was introduced to The Beatles by Robert Fraser, art gallery owner and friend of The Rolling Stones. The artwork fused the two worlds of Pop Art and Rock Music.

**3**| Where: 18 Redburn Street
Who: **BOB GELDOF**
When: Mid 1980s-1996

Home to Bob Geldof who started **Band Aid** and Live Aid. He wrote, with Midge Ure of Ultravox, the charity single *Do They Know It's Christmas?,* the biggest selling single in Britain.

Geldof was moved to raise funds for Africa when Paula Yates left a note on the fridge door of their previous house in south Clapham, telling him to 'do something' after news reports of droughts in Ethiopia.

Yates lives in this house with her new partner, Michael Hutchence of INXS. Geldof lives in Hutchence's old mews house off Cheyne Walk.

**3 Cheyne Walk** home to Keith Richards during the late 1960s

**4** | Where: 3 Cheyne Walk
Who: **KEITH RICHARDS-THE ROLLING STONES**
When: Late 1960s

Keith Richards bought this mansion overlooking the Thames in the late 1960s. He lived here for some years with girlfriend Anita Pallenburg. On the first floor he created an Arab interior where he would stay for days at a time, taking drugs and composing music.

**5** | Where: Oakley Street
Who: **DAVID BOWIE**
When: 1973

David Bowie lived here with wife Angie when they moved back into central London from Kent. On 17 November 1973, the American writer William Burroughs visited Bowie at his house. His work, and that of George Orwell's '1984', inspired the *Diamond Dogs* album that Bowie wrote whilst living here.

**6** | Where: 48 Cheyne Walk
Who: **MICK JAGGER-THE ROLLING STONES**
When: 1967 onwards

Mick Jagger bought this house, down the road from Keith Richards, in 1967. Both girlfriend Marianne Faithfull and wife Bianca Jagger have lived here with him.

Jagger built a studio in the garden and many songs were written there, including his contribution to the *Let It Bleed* album. The song *You Can't Always Get What You Want* was written about the local Chelsea Drugs Store, at 49 King's Road.

*Sympathy For The Devil* was inspired by Faithfull reading 'The Master and Margarita', a Faustian drama by Mikhail Bulgakov. She has described Jagger's song as "pure papier maché Satanism". It was withdrawn from *Let It Bleed* by Decca, allowing Faithfull to record it first.

Jagger wrote *Sister Morphine* with Faithfull in their bedroom in the house.

The house witnessed some incidents with the police: Jagger was arrested with Faithfull at the house on 24 May 1969 for drug possession and a court order was taken out by his estranged wife, Bianca, to prevent him entering the house until their divorce was finalised in 1980.

It was nearby at 100 Cheyne Walk, the home of friend Christopher Gibb, that Jagger met Marianne Faithfull at a party.

**48 Cheyne Walk**
Home to Mick Jagger from 1967

**7** | Where: 245A King's Road, Chelsea Antiques Market
When: 1960s-1980s

**ONOVAN** wrote *Jennifer Juniper*, inspired by Jenny Boyd who had a stall here lled Juniper with her sister, Patti Boyd (wife of both George Harrison and Eric apton). They gave up the stall in 1969 because of the early morning starts.

Donovan wrote many songs inspired by London locations: for example, *Sunny odge Street* was about the street off Tottenham Court Road, famed in the 60s for its cafes and drugs.

*Mellow Yellow* was his first major US hit produced by Mickie Most and arranged by John Paul Jones, later of Led Zeppelin. The background whispering was by Paul McCartney, a favour Donovan returned on *Yellow Submarine*. And...

**BOY GEORGE** worked in the market in the early 1980s on a stall called Shades.

**8** | Where: 46A Old Church Street, Sound Techniques Studio
Who: **PINK FLOYD**
When: 1967

Pink Floyd recorded their first single *Arnold Layne* at these studios on 27 February 1967. It was produced by Joe Boyd, a founder of the UFO Club on Tottenham Court Road.

To promote their music, Pink Floyd decided to give up college for a year.

They recorded *See Emily Play* here on 23 May 1967. This had been written by Syd Barrett for their concert on 12 May at the Queen Elizabeth Hall. The concert was the first time a quadraphonic PA system was used, creating four-way stereo sound and it was called 'Games for May'. They advertised it as a liquid light show: "Space-age relaxation for the climax of spring - electronic compositions, colour and image projections, girls and The Pink Floyd."

Dave Gilmour dropped in to see the band whilst they were recording at the studios in 1967. He was a friend of Roger Water's from Cambridge. Gilmour joined Pink Floyd in January 1968 just before Barrett left.

**9** | Where: 44 Old Church Street
Who: **DEF LEPPARD-STEVE CLARK**
When: 8 January 1991

Steve Clark, the guitarist of Def Leppard, died of an overdose of drugs and alcohol in his flat here. The group were at the height of their commercial success after releasing *Hysteria*, which exceeded the five million sales of the previous album, *Pyromania*.

**36A OLD CHURCH STREET** HOME OF ER
CLAPTON

**10** | Where: 36a Old Church Street
Who: **ERIC CLAPTON**
When: 1990s

This is the Chelsea home of Eric Clapton, where he moved after selling Hurtwood Edge in Surrey. Whilst staying here he frequently visits the Chelsea Arts Club, also in Old Church Street.

**11** | Where: Danvers Street
Who: **MARIANNE FAITHFULL**
When: 1979

Marianne Faithfull lived in a flat just off the King's Road whilst she wrote her album, *Broken English*. She worked on the songs with husband Ben Brierly.

**12** | Where: 430 King's Road, Sex
Who: **THE SEX PISTOLS**
When: October 1975

Shop owned by Malcolm McLaren and Vivienne Westwood in the mid 1970s.

McLaren had been living in New York where he had briefly managed the New York Dolls. Back in England he and Westwood began selling Teddy Boy outfits with a bondage influence, inspired by Richard Hell and his proto-punk group, Television. They had developed the look of Vaseline-spiked hair and clothes held together with safety pins.

Using regulars to the shop, McLaren decided to create a group to promote the clothes. Glen Matlock was a shop assistant, as were school friends, Paul Cook and Steve Jones.

**SEX AT 430 KING'S ROAD** BIRTHPLACE OF THE SEX PISTOLS

When the green-haired Johnny Rotten came into the shop McLaren asked him to audition. Though barely able to sing, his attitude was perfect and The Sex Pistols were born.

Also…

**THE PRETENDERS'** Chrissie Hynde worked at the shop for a short time in early 1974.

Also…

**THE CLASH's** manager, Bernie Rhodes, worked at Sex as McLaren's assistant in the mid-seventies.

Across the road was Granny Takes A Trip, a shop stocking psychedelic clothes and popular with Pink Floyd, T Rex and The Faces.

**13** | Where: 500 King's Road, Wetherby Arms Pub (now Tiger Lils)
Who: **THE ROLLING STONES-BILL WYMAN**
When: 7 December 1962

Bill Wyman auditioned for The Rolling Stones in a room at the pub where the group used to practise. Though they initially thought him too old, they were impressed by his car and, more particularly, his amplifiers.

Wyman's debut with the band was at St Mary's Church Hall, Putney on 15 December 1962.

**14** | Where: 102 Edith Grove
Who: **THE ROLLING STONES**
When: Late 1962-63

Brian Jones lived in the middle floor flat when the group first formed.

Keith Richards and Mick Jagger joined him in late 1962 to share the rent. The flat was in a terrible state. They were not earning any money and they survived on Jagger's student grant cheque supplemented by food hand outs from Bill Wyman and Richards' mother.

Whilst Jagger attended college, Jones and Richards spent the winter huddled together developing the twin lead guitar-style of The Stones.

It was at Edith Grove that Jagger's stage personality evolved through, amongst other things, his experimentation with makeup and female clothes: a sight that horrified the visiting John Lennon.

**102 Edith Grove**

**15** | Where: 11 Gunter Grove
Who: **TIM RICE**
When: Mid 1960s

Tim Rice lived here whilst writing the lyrics to *Joseph And His Amazing Technicolor Dreamcoat* and *Jesus Christ Superstar*.

**16** | Where: 45 Gunter Grove
Who: **PUBLIC IMAGE LIMITED**
When: 1978-early 1981

After The Sex Pistols split up, Rotten reverted to his real name of John Lydon and formed PIL. However the notoriety of The Sex Pistols followed him and neighbours often called the police to the house for alleged public disturbances.

PIL began in April 1978 with ex-Clash Keith Levene, friend Jah Wobble and Jim Walker. By the late 1980s, only Lydon of the original group, remained.

**17** | Where: 266 Fulham Road, Café Des Artistes
Who: **STATUS QUO**
When: 1965

Status Quo, as fifteen year olds calling themselves The Spectres, had their first residency here. The group had formed at Sedgehill Comprehensive in Bellingham, south-east London. Their live debut was at the Samuel Jones Sports Club in Dulwich in 1962, near ATC HQ on Lordship Lane where they rehearsed.

Status Quo are the most successful UK chart group after The Beatles.

**18** | Where: 3a Seymour Walk, The Priory
Who: **LIONEL BART**
When: 1965-1968

Lionel Bart was born Lionel Begleiter in Brick Lane, east London.

Bart was a prolific composer of hits in the 1950s and 1960s after leaving St Martin's School of Art. In 1956, he won an Ivor Novello Award for the Tommy Steele hit *Little White Bull*. Later he wrote *Living Doll* for Cliff Richard. His greatest success was in the sixties when he wrote the stage musical 'Oliver!'.

Despite his vast song royalties, Bart's extravagant lifestyle led to bankruptcy in 1968.

**19** | Where: 25 Holmead Road
Who: **MARC BOLAN**
When: 1976

Marc Bolan lived at this house shortly before his death in a car-accident in Barnes. Whilst living here, he had planned his comeback, but it never happened.

**20** | Where: Chelsea Harbour, Conrad Hotel
When: 1990s

A favourite location for stars performing in London because of its convenience to Heathrow and Earl's Court. Recent guests have included Prince, Neil Diamond and David Bowie. Take That were told to stay elsewhere when their teenage fans made a nuisance of themselves, making bookings to stay at the hotel.

Elton John used to live in the penthouse of the residential Belvedere Tower in the late 1980s. He sold the flat in the mid-1990s for £1.1 million.

THE GARDEN WALL AT **1 LOGAN PLACE** THE LAST HOME OF FREDDIE MERCURY OF QUEEN

WITH LOVE BY
MARIA
I STILL LOVE YOU
MEXICO
I still love you
We love you FREDDIE
KAROL
4.6.93
FREDDIE

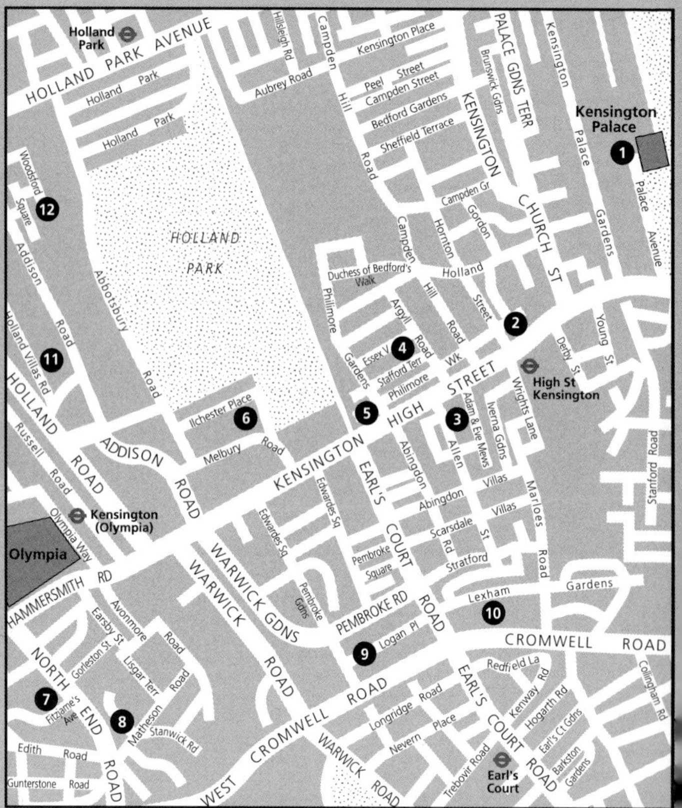

Holland Park
HOLLAND PARK AVENUE
Holland Park
Holland Park
Hillsleigh Rd
Aubrey Road
Campden Hill Road
Kensington Place
Peel Street
Campden Street
Bedford Gardens
Sheffield Terrace
Brunswick Gdns
PALACE GDNS TERR
KENSINGTON CHURCH ST
Kensington Palace Gardens
Kensington Palace
Palace Avenue
1
Woodsford Square
12
HOLLAND PARK
Addison Road
Abbotsbury Road
Campden Gr
Gordon
Hornton Street
Campden Hill
Holland Street
Duchess of Bedford's Walk
Phillimore Gardens
Argyll Road
Hill Road
Wk
Young St
Derby St
2
Holland Villas Rd
11
HOLLAND ROAD
Russell Road
Essex V
4
Stafford Terr
Phillimore
High St Kensington
Wrights Lane
Stanford Road
Ilchester Place
6
5
HIGH STREET
3
Adam & Eve Mews
Iverna Gdns
ADDISON ROAD
Melbury Road
KENSINGTON
EARL'S COURT ROAD
Abingdon
Allen
Edwardes Sq
Abingdon Villas
Villas
Marloes Road
Kensington (Olympia)
Olympia Way
Olympia
Scarsdale
Rd
St
Pembroke Square
Stratford
HAMMERSMITH RD
WARWICK GDNS
WARWICK
Pembroke Gdns
PEMBROKE RD
Lexham Gardens
10
Earsby St
Avonmore Road
Logan Pl
9
CROMWELL ROAD
Redfield La
Gorleston St
NORTH END ROAD
Lisgar Terr
Road
ROAD
Kenway Rd
Collingham Rd
Hogarth Rd
7
Fitzjame's Ave
8
Matheson Road
Stanwick Rd
WEST CROMWELL ROAD
Longridge Road
Nevern Place
Earl's Ct Gdns
EARL'S COURT ROAD
Barkston Gardens
Edith Road
Gunterstone Road
WARWICK ROAD
Trebovir Road
Earl's Court

# Kensington W8|14



**1**| Where: Kensington Palace, Old Barracks
Who: **GENESIS-PETER GABRIEL**
When: 1971

Peter Gabriel frequently stayed at this flat, home to the parents of Jill, his first wife.

One night with friends, whilst discussing good versus evil, Gabriel took LSD. The 24 minute song, *Supper's Ready*, on the *Foxtrot* album, was inspired by the experience.

**2**| Where: 74d Kensington High Street
Who: **MICK FLEETWOOD-FLEETWOOD MAC**
When: 1968

Mick Fleetwood lived here in 1968 when Fleetwood Mac released their debut album, *Fleetwood Mac*. Songs on the album included *Black Magic Woman* and *Need Your Love So Bad*.

**3**| Where: Adam & Eve Mews
Who: **GEORGE MICHAEL**
When: 1985

George Michael rented a flat in this mews street at the height of Wham!'s success during the release of *Careless Whisper*.

**4**| Where: 12 Stafford Terrace
Who: **FREDDIE MERCURY-QUEEN**
When: Mid 1980s

Freddie Mercury lived here in the mid-1980s before moving to Logan Place.

**5**| Where: 1A Philimore Gardens, Sticky Fingers
Who: **BILL WYMAN**
When: 17 May 1989

Bill Wyman opened the restaurant shortly before his brief marriage to Mandy Smith. The walls contain mementoes of The Stones' career from Wyman's exhaustive collection. Wyman left The Stones in 1993 and has a personal wealth of approximately £35 million.

**6**| Where: 29 Melbury Road, Tower House
Who: **JIMMY PAGE-LED ZEPPELIN**
When: 3 April 1974

mmy Page bought this house from actor Richard Harris. Each room in the othic towered house has a different decorative style.

After the break-up of Led Zeppelin, Page composed the music for the film Death Wish II', as a favour to his neighbour, the director Michael Winner.

Page had previously lived at Plumpton Place in Plumpton, Sussex and at the Old ill House in Windsor. He bought the Old Mill House from Michael Caine and it as there that Led Zeppelin drummer John Bonham died during rehearsals in ptember 1980.

**29 Melbury Road** home to Jimmy Page, ex-Led Zeppelin

Jimmy Page and Robert Plant, who lives near Primrose Hill, are each worth £45 million, from their time with Led Zeppelin.

**7** | Where: Fitzjames Avenue, Fitzjames Mansions
Who: **THE ANIMALS**
When: 1964

The Animals lived in a furniture-less flat here when they first moved to London.

They had signed a contract with record producer Mickie Most, who then got them the deal with EMI. At the time they were playing sessions at The Marquee.

**8** | Where: 171 North End Road, Nashville Rooms
Who: **THE SEX PISTOLS**
When: 1976

A popular music venue of the 1970s.

Though Johnny Rotten wrote most of the lyrics for *Pretty Vacant*, Glen Matlock wrote his share of the lyrics during a sound check for a Sex Pistols gig here. He had written the music previously at Moonies Bar in Covent Garden.

**9** | Where: 1 Logan Place
Who: **FREDDIE MERCURY-QUEEN**
When: Mid 1980s-1991

Lead singer of Queen, Freddie Mercury (real name Frederick Bulsara) lived here from the mid-1980s until his death. He bought the house for its privacy and the long garden wall has become a graffiti shrine for fans from around the world.

Mercury said about his music:

> " My songs are like Bic razors. For fun, for modern consumption. You listen to it, like it, discard it, then go on to the next. Disposable pop."

Not long before his death from AIDS, he remarked that he would find it boring to live to seventy. He also added:

> "I'd like to be buried with all my treasures, just like the Pharaohs. If I could afford it, I'd have a pyramid built in Kensington."

**10** | Where: 81 Lexham Gardens
Who: **MARC BOLAN**
When: 1961

When only 14 years old, Bolan left school (Hill Croft School, Beechcroft Road, Earlsfield) to live in Central London. He appeared on an ITV children's show, 'The Five O'clock Club' and lived in a flat here with the show's presenter, Allen Warren.

Soon afterwards, Bolan recorded his first single, the unsuccessful *You're No Good*, using the name Toby Tyler.

Tony Visconti, David Bowie's record producer, lived at 108 Lexham Gardens. He became the producer of Tyrannosaurus Rex (T Rex) in 1968. Bolan rehearsed and wrote *Debora*, T Rex's first single, in Visconti's flat.

**11** | Where: 35 Holland Villas Road
Who: **SUPERTRAMP**
When: 1973

Communal house used by Supertramp when writing songs in the early 1970s.

The hit single *Breakfast In America* was written in the house as well as material for their first hit album *Crime Of The Century*.

Supertramp formed in 1969 but it was not until 1973 when they lived in Holland Villas Road that the final line-up of the band was put together.

**12** | Where: 2 Woodsford Square
Who: **THE STYLE COUNCIL**
When: 1996

London home to Paul Weller after the break-up of The Style Council.

Weller had formed The Style Council when The Jam split. The Style Council were initially successful, even owning the Solid Bond studios near Marble Arch. However, financial losses caused Weller to face bankruptcy and the sale of the studios.

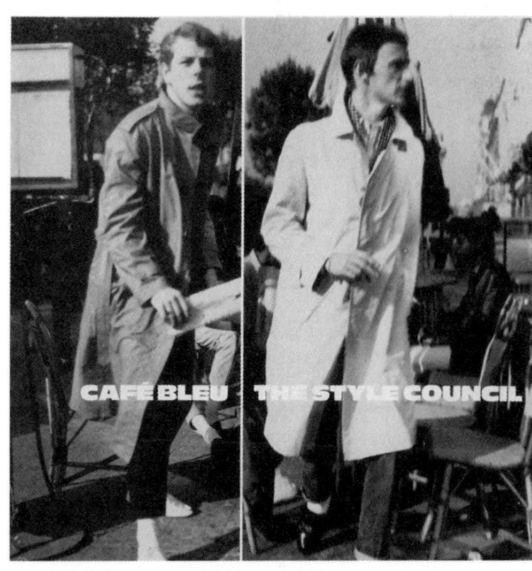

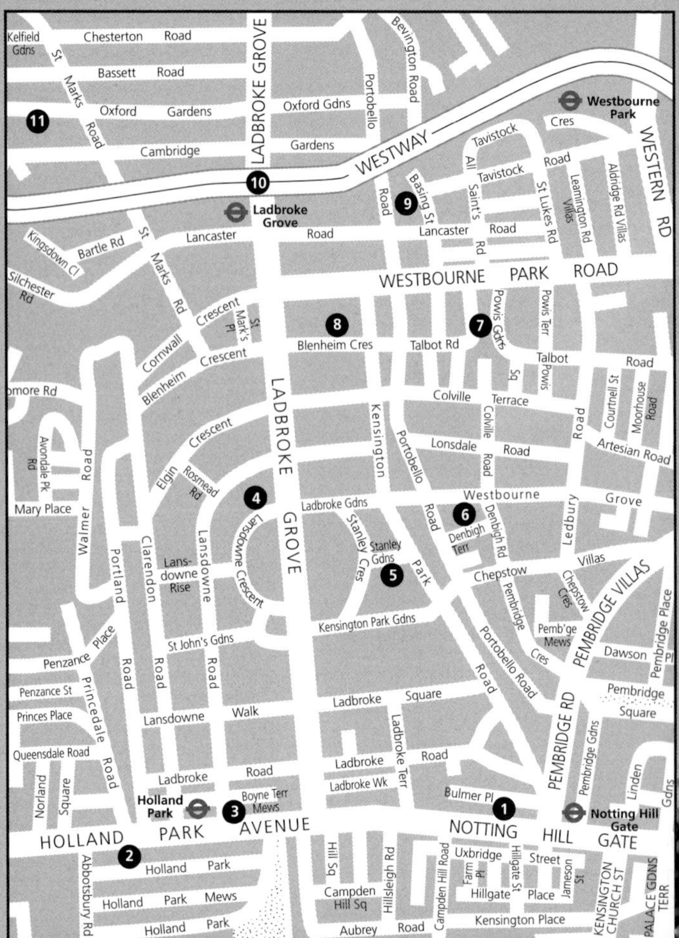

Kelfield Gdns
Chesterton Road
Bassett Road
St Marks Road
Oxford Gardens
Cambridge Gardens
LADBROKE GROVE
Oxford Gdns
Portobello Road
Bevington Road
WESTWAY
Westbourne Park
Tavistock Cres
Tavistock Road
All Saint's Rd
Basing St
St Lukes Rd
Leamington Rd Villas
Aldridge Rd Villas
WESTERN RD
Ladbroke Grove
Lancaster Road
Kingsdown Cl
Bartle Rd
Silchester Rd
Marks Rd
St Mark's Pl
Crescent
WESTBOURNE PARK ROAD
Powis Gdns
Powis Terr
Blenheim Cres
Talbot Rd
Talbot Road
Cornwall Crescent
Blenheim Crescent
Powis Sq
Colville Terrace
Colville Road
Courtnell St
Moorhouse Road
Artesian Road
Lonsdale Road
Kensington Park Road
Portobello
Avondale Pk Rd
Walmer Road
Elgin Crescent
Rosmead Rd
Mary Place
Westbourne Grove
Ladbroke Gdns
Stanley Cres
Stanley Gdns
Denbigh Terr
Denbigh Rd
Ledbury Road
Clarendon Road
Lansdowne Rise
Lansdowne Road
Lansdowne Crescent
Portland Road
Chepstow Villas
Chepstow Cres
Pembridge Cres
Pemb'ge Mews
PEMBRIDGE VILLAS
Pembridge Place
Kensington Park Gdns
St John's Gdns
Penzance Place
Penzance St
Princedale Road
Princes Place
Portobello Road
Dawson Pl
Pembridge Square
Ladbroke Square
Lansdowne Walk
Queensdale Road
Norland Square
Ladbroke Road
Ladbroke Terr
PEMBRIDGE RD
Pembridge Gdns
Linden Gdns
Ladbroke Wk
Bulmer Pl
Holland Park
Boyne Terr Mews
Notting Hill Gate
HOLLAND PARK AVENUE
NOTTING HILL GATE
Abbotsbury Rd
Holland Park
Holland Park Mews
Hill Sq
Campden Hill Sq
Hillsleigh Rd
Campden Hill Road
Uxbridge Street
Farm Pl
Hillgate St
Hillgate Place
Jameson St
KENSINGTON CHURCH ST
PALACE GDNS TERR
Aubrey Road
Kensington Place
1
2
3
4
5
6
7
8
9
10
11

## Notting Hill W10 | 11



**1** | Where: Notting Hill Gate, Campden Hill Towers
Who: **TOM JONES**
When: 11 March 1965

Home of Tom Jones's first manager, Gordon Mills. He lived in a council flat above McDonalds where he co-wrote the massive hit *It's Not Unusual* with Les Reed.

The song was turned down by Sandie Shaw, allowing Thomas Woodward (who soon changed his name to Tom Jones) to launch his career. The demo was recorded by Jones in Denmark Street.

**2** | Where: 81 Holland Park, Halcyon Hotel
Who: **OASIS & IGGY POP**
When: 1990s

The cover photograph for the Oasis single, *Cigarettes And Alcohol,* was taken in this hotel. Iggy Pop often stays at the Halcyon when in London.

**3** | Where: Lansdowne Road, Lansdowne House Studios
Who: **THE SEX PISTOLS**
When: Summer 1976

The Pistols recorded *Anarchy In The UK* here. It was banned because of alleged racial references. The resulting furore caused EMI to cancel their contract, not wishing to continue apologising for the group's behaviour.

During breaks in the recording, The Pistols wrote *God Save The Queen*.

**4** | Where: 21-22 Lansdowne Crescent, Samarkand Hotel
Who: **JIMI HENDRIX**
When: 17-18 September 1970

Jimi Hendrix took a fatal overdose here, in the basement flat owned by his girlfriend, Monika Danneneden. He died at the Great Cumberland Hotel on Oxford Street.

**21-22 Lansdowne Crescent**

Stanley Gardens

**5** | Where: 22 Stanley Gardens, Portobello Hotel
When: 1990s

**BLUR's** singer Damon Albarn was a barman at the hotel in 1990 when the group made their first demo for Food Records at the Powerhouse Studios. He was also studying drama at the East 15 School. At fifteen, Albarn had won the regional young composer of the year award and, before he joined Blur, had been offered a solo contract.

And...

Oasis, Pulp, Suede, Seal, U2, Mick Jagger, George Michael and Axl Rose have all stayed at the hotel. It is convenient for both Wembley and Earls Court.

Also...

**TINA TURNER** used to live in the house next door and **PULP's** Jarvis Cocker lives in nearby Ladbroke Grove.

**6** | Where: 19 Denbigh Terrace
Who: **RICHARD BRANSON**
When: 1974

Richard Branson lived here when he signed Mike Oldfield's *Tubular Bells* to the Virgin label. Thus he laid the foundations for Virgin's success.

All Saints' Church
in Powis Gardens

**7** | Where: Powis Gardens, All Saints' Church Hall
When: 1960s

**PINK FLOYD** had a residency at the London Free School's Light & Sound workshops, held in the church hall in October 1966. The School was a spin off from the magazine, The International Times, and helped to arrange the first Notting Hill Carnival. Pink Floyd played many benefits for IT, including twice at Alexandra Palace.

During the workshops Pink Floyd composed *Interstellar Overdrive*, *Stoned Alone* and *Astronomy Domini*. They also developed their light show and slide projections.

EMI saw the group playing here and offered a recording contract.

And...

**HAWKWIND** played their first concert here under the name, Group X. Hawkwind were attached to the Notting Hill area, naming an album after a café on Portobello Road, the Mountain Grill.

**8** | Where: Blenheim Crescent
When: 1960s-1990s

**MARC BOLAN** lived at No.57 in 1967 when forming T Rex. Bolan wrote *Ride A White Swan* there.

And...

**THE POLICE's** manager, Miles Copeland, lived at No.41B for many years.

**Sarm Studios**

**9** | Where: 8 Basing Street, Sarm Studios West
When: 1970s-1990s

**LED ZEPPELIN** recorded parts of *Led Zeppelin IV* here in December 1970, including the electronic section of *Stairway To Heaven*.

*Stairway to Heaven* started life in a cottage at Bron-Yr-Aur in Wales. Jimmy Page wrote the acoustic introduction there. The lyrics and the rest came at Basing Street, with the song completed at Headley Grange Studios in Hampshire. Jimmy Page described the recording:

> "For some reason we decided to take the Stones mobile truck there ... It seemed ideal - as soon as we thought of an idea, we put it down on tape. ... The only thing wrong was that we'd get so excited about an idea that we'd really rush to finish its format to get it on tape."

He recognised that *Stairway To Heaven* was important for Led Zeppelin:

"We were careful not to release it as a single. It was a milestone for us. Every musician wants to do something of lasting quality, something that will hold up for a long time and I guess we did it with *Stairway.*"

Also on the album was *Black Dog* about which Page said:

"Not all my stuff is meant to be scrutinised. Things like *Black Dog* are blatant let's-do-it-in-the-bath type things, but they make their point just the same. People listen. Otherwise, you might as well sing the menu from the Continental Hyatt."

And so was *Rock 'N' Roll*, described by Page as a "spontaneous combustion".

Also...

**FRANKIE GOES TO HOLLYWOOD** were signed up by Trevor Horn for ZTT records, after a failed deal with Arista. They recorded their first LP *Welcome To The Pleasure Dome* here in 1984.

And...

**BAND AID** recorded the most famous charity record here on 25 November 1984. *Do They Know Its Christmas?* was written by Bob Geldof and Midge Ure of Ultravox. It went straight to No.1 in the UK when released and sold over three million, the biggest ever selling single in the UK.

And...

**GEORGE MICHAEL** wrote songs for *Older* when recording the album at the studios in late 1995.

**10** | Where: The Westway
Who: **THE CLASH**
When: August Bank Holiday 1976

Mick Jones wrote *White Riot* after seeing the riots and violence at the Notting Hill Carnival of 1976. The song told 'whites' to rise up against the system, like the blacks had done at the carnival.

The Clash had their photo taken underneath the Westway, early in 1977, as a back shot for the forthcoming debut album, *The Clash*.

Guitarist Mick Jones lived with his grandmother on the nineteenth floor of Wilmcote House on the Warwick and Brindley Estate, Woodchester Square. The influence of the Westway area is reflected in his songs.

Joe Strummer also knew the area well, having worked for Robertino's Ice Cream Factory in Foscote Mews before forming his first group, the 101ers, based at a squat at 101 Warburton Terrace in East London.

**The Jam**, in 1977, used the same Westway setting as The Clash for the cover of their second album, *This Is The Modern World*.

**11** | Where: 95 Oxford Gardens
Who: **HEAVEN 17**
When: Early 1980s

Glenn Gregory lived here after leaving the Human League and Sheffield.

With Martyn Ware and Ian Craig-Marsh, he established the British Electric Foundation with Heaven 17 as their first project. The group's most successful albums were *Penthouse And Pavement* and *The Luxury Gap*.

As producers, they worked with Tina Turner and re-launched her career as a solo artist.

## Bayswater W2

**1** | Where: 61 Edgware Road, The Lotus House
Who: **THE KINKS**
When: 31 December 1963

The Kinks played their first professional gig at this restaurant.

They had just signed a management contract with Robert Wace and Grenville Collins in September, after playing at Hornsey Town Hall.

Wace changed their name from The Ravens to The Kinks in November, after the 'kinkiness' of the decade.

**2** | Where: Park West Place
Who: **MARVIN GAYE**
When: 1980

Marvin Gaye stayed at a flat here to escape the stresses of his life in the US. Amongst other problems, he was going through his second divorce and the IRS were chasing him for unpaid tax.

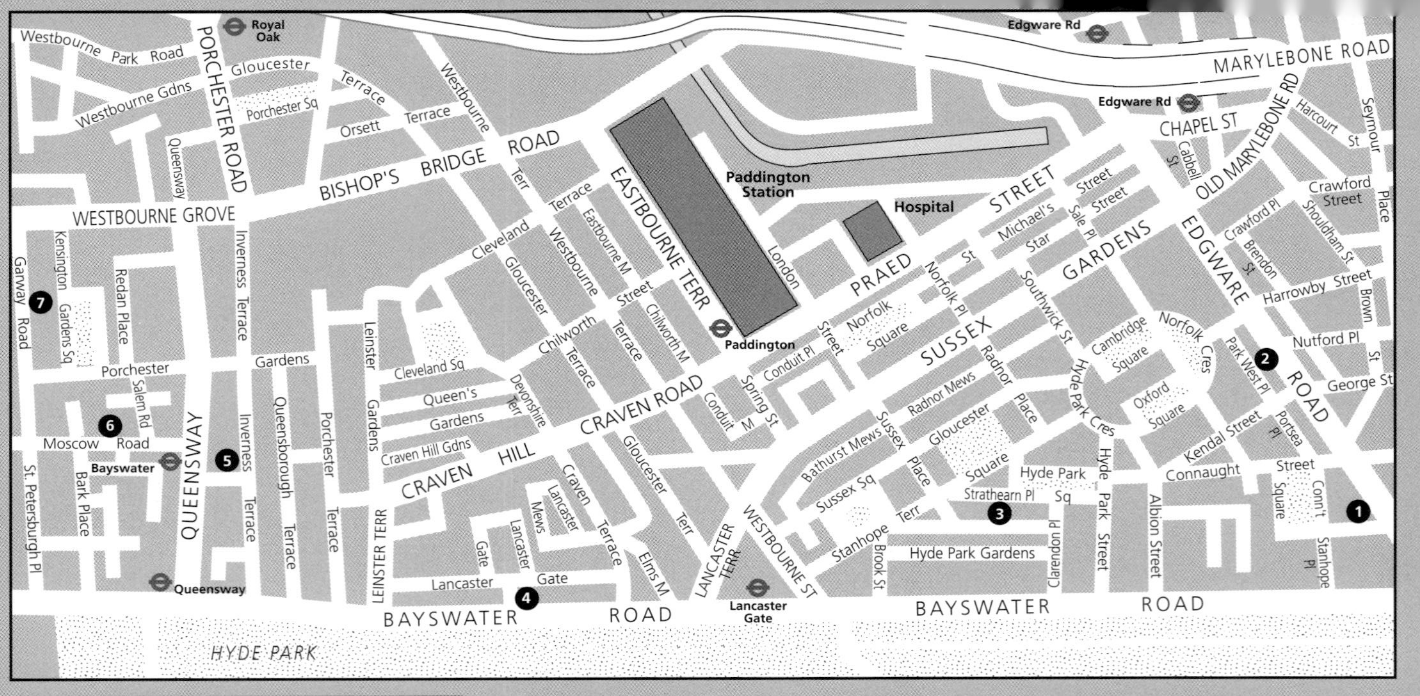
Royal Oak
Westbourne Park Road
PORCHESTER ROAD
Gloucester Terrace
Westbourne Gdns
Porchester Sq
Orsett Terrace
Westbourne Terrace
Queensway
BISHOP'S BRIDGE ROAD
WESTBOURNE GROVE
Kensington Gardens Sq
Garway Road
Redan Place
Inverness Terrace
Porchester
Salem Rd
Moscow Road
Bayswater
QUEENSWAY
Queensborough Terrace
Porchester Terrace
Gardens
Leinster Gardens
St. Petersburgh Pl
Bark Place
Queensway
Cleveland Sq
Queen's Gardens
Craven Hill Gdns
Devonshire Terr
Cleveland Gloucester Terrace
Terr
Eastbourne M
Chilworth Street
Chilworth M
Chilworth Terrace
EASTBOURNE TERR
Paddington
Paddington Station
Hospital
London Street
PRAED STREET
Norfolk Square
Norfolk Pl
Conduit Pl
Spring St
Conduit M
CRAVEN ROAD
CRAVEN HILL
LEINSTER TERR
Lancaster Gate
Lancaster Mews
Craven Terrace
Gloucester Terr
Elms M
LANCASTER TERR
WESTBOURNE ST
Lancaster Gate
BAYSWATER ROAD
HYDE PARK
SUSSEX GARDENS
Radnor Mews
Radnor Place
Bathurst Mews
Sussex Place
Sussex Sq
Gloucester Square
Stanhope Terr
Brook St
Hyde Park Gardens
Strathearn Pl
Hyde Park Sq
Clarendon Pl
Hyde Park Street
Hyde Park Cres
Southwick St
Star Street
Michael's Street
Sale Pl
St
Cambridge Square
Oxford Square
Norfolk Cres
Albion Street
Connaught Street
Conn't Square
Stanhope Pl
Kendal Street
Portsea Pl
Park West Pl
EDGWARE ROAD
George St
Nutford Pl
Brown St
Harrowby Street
Brendon St
Crawford Pl
Shouldham St
Crawford Street
Place
Seymour
Harcourt St
OLD MARYLEBONE RD
Cabbell St
CHAPEL ST
Edgware Rd
MARYLEBONE ROAD
1
2
3
4
5
6
7

3 | Where: 2 Strathearn Place, Flat 1
Who: **THE BEATLES**
When: 1965

George Harrison and John Lennon sampled LSD for the first time here, at the home of Harrison's dentist. This led to a more experimental approach to The Beatles' music, reflected in the song *Strawberry Fields* and the *Sergeant Pepper* and *Revolver* albums.

4 | Where: 95 Lancaster Gate, Columbia Hotel
When: 1980s & 1990s

This residential hotel has been used by many groups when they first come to London.

**Julian Cope and The Teardrop Explodes** were the first group to stay here in 1983.

**Oasis** were more recent visitors in summer 1994, trashing a room in traditional pop star style. They were the first group to be banned from the hotel. They remembered the hotel in the title of their early song, *Columbia*.

5 | Where: 41-49 Inverness Terrace, Hyde Park Towers
Who: **JIMI HENDRIX**
When: September 1966

Jimi Hendrix stayed here for the first few nights on his arrival in London.

He had been brought over from New York by his manager and ex-Animals' bassist, Chas Chandler.

6 | Where: Moscow Road
When: 1960s

**THE ROLLING STONES'** Brian Jones lived with **Alexis Korner**, of Blues Incorporated, at 4 Burnham Court on Moscow Road.

They had met in Cheltenham, Jones' hometown, and Korner, a leading influence in London's Blues development, invited Jones to stay when he came to London in early 1962. Jones spent much time at the flat becoming familiar with the emerging Blues scene.

He also worked at Whiteley's Department Store nearby when he formed The Rolling Stones. But he was sacked from the job for stealing equipment for the group.

Also...

**CROSBY, STILLS & NASH** rehearsed in a house on Moscow Road from August to December 1968 when the three came to England to launch themselves as a trio.

Stephen Stills (Buffalo Springfield), David Crosby (The Byrds) and Graham Nash (The Hollies) decided to form a group after meeting in the US.

7 | Where: 12 Garway Road
Who: **SINEAD O'CONNOR**
When: 1990s

Dublin-born Sinead O'Connor lives in the house with the pink door, when in London.

In 1992 she donated her $800,000 Californian home to the Red Cross for their Somalia appeal.

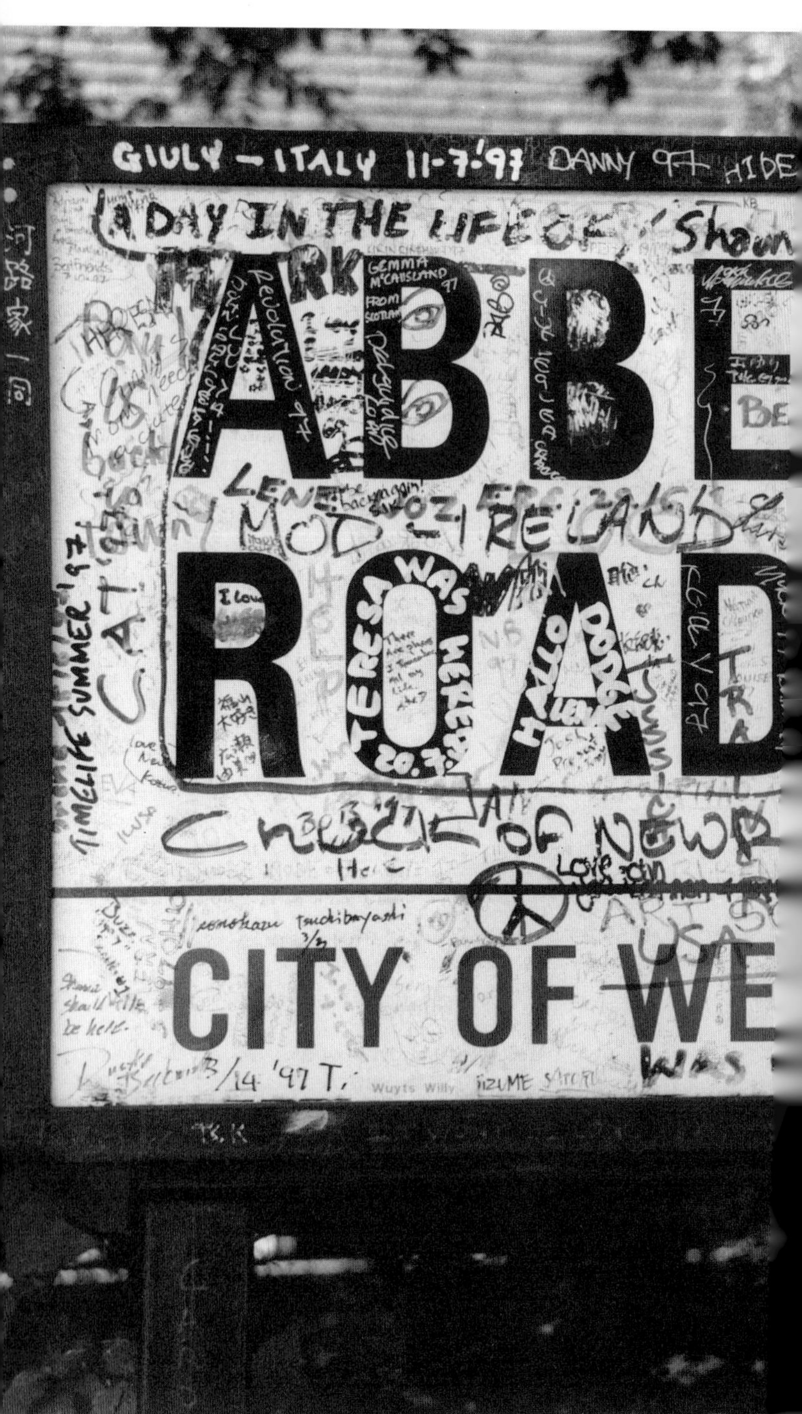


**Abbey Road** home to the studios in St John's Wood, North-west London

ERE WILL NEVER BE ANOTHER BEATLES
NW8
MINSTER
I LOVE PAUL!
I saw her standing there
Junko Adachi
COOL SIGN

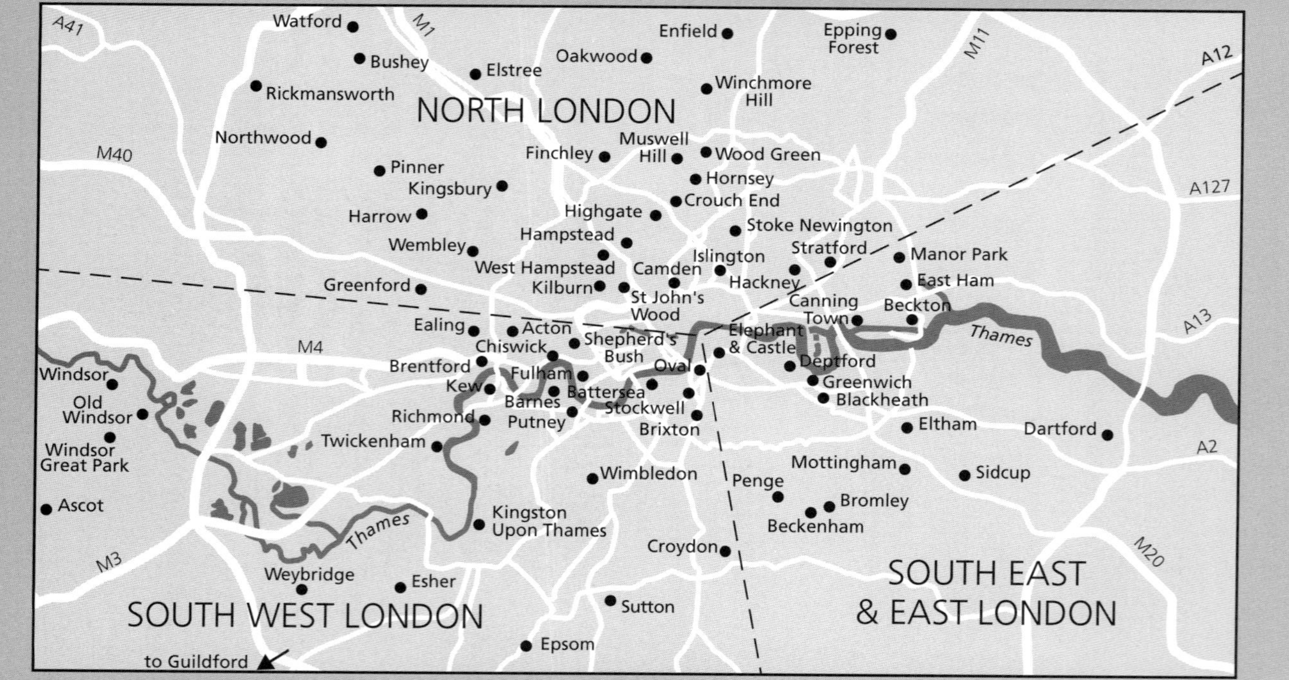


## Greater & Outer London

# St John's Wood NW8

**1** | Where: 3 Abbey Road, Abbey Road Studios
When: 1960s-1990s

The most important recording studio in Rock & Pop history. Nearly every successful musician has played here at some time, from the auditioning Cliff Richard to the young hopefuls of today.

There are three main studios at Abbey Road, of which No.2 is perhaps the most famous.

**CLIFF RICHARD** auditioned for the EMI record label at the studios on 19 August 1958 after a talent contest at the Gaumont Cinema on Shepherd's Bush Green.

The Shadows, when still called The Drifters, also auditioned for EMI here, and soon released their first single *Feelin' Fine*.

And...

**THE BEATLES'** first recording session took place here on 6 June 1962.

They were performing in Hamburg and were told of the recording offer in a telegram from their manager Brian Epstein. Epstein sent it from the Post Office on Wellington Road next to St John's Wood tube station.

The session was an audition for EMI and Pete Best was still the drummer. However, when they returned on 11 September 1962 to record four songs, including their own compositions, *PS I Love You* and *Love Me Do*, Best had been replaced by Ringo Starr.

Producer George Martin, shocked at the change and doubtful of Starr's talent, hired a session drummer. Starr was allowed only to play maracas and tambourine.

The Beatles recorded their first album, *Please Please Me*, in 12 hours.

The large No.2 studio became their main recording base throughout their career.

**CHRIS REA** has said that all musicians, after a successful first album, want to use Studio 2 for their second album, as they hope its history will reflect on their success.

Around the corner from the studios, on the junction with Grove End Road, the four Beatles were photographed on the pedestrian crossing for the cover of their second to last album, *Abbey Road*. The photo was taken on 8 August 1969 during a 10 minute photo session by Iain Macmillan.

And...
**PINK FLOYD** recorded their first album *Piper At The Gates of Dawn* here, coincidentally at the same time as The Beatles were recording *Sergeant Pepper's Lonely Hearts Club Band* in May 1967. Pink Floyd recorded many other early albums here, including *Dark Side of the Moon*.
And...
**ELTON JOHN** played the piano on The Hollies' *He Ain't Heavy He's My Brother*, recorded at the studios on 25 June 1967.

The influence of Abbey Road's history continues today, when allegedly the Gallagher brothers of **Oasis** moved to neighbouring streets to be near the musical centre of their heroes, The Beatles.

**2** | Where: Garden Road
Who: **THE BEATLES-PAUL McCARTNEY**
When: 23 February 1967

Working around Abbey Road Studios was the traffic warden, Meta Davis.

One day Paul McCartney's car was ticketed and he wrote *Lovely Rita* in response.

John Lennon regarded the song as boring, because it was about normal people doing normal things.

**7 CAVENDISH AVENUE** THE LONDON HOME OF PAUL MCCARTNEY SINCE 1966

**3** | Where: 7 Cavendish Avenue
Who: **PAUL McCARTNEY**
When: 1966-1990s

This house, around the corner from the Abbey Road Studios, was bought by Paul McCartney in 1966 for £40,000. Formerly he had lived at the home of Jane Asher in Wimpole Street. Asher briefly lived with him here until McCartney met Linda Eastman and they split up.

Most of his late sixties songs were written at Cavendish Avenue, including *Penny Lane*, *Helter-Skelter* and *Sergeant Pepper*. *Blackbird* was written early one summer morning in the garden and *Martha My Dear* whilst watching his Old English Sheep dog, Martha, running around.

McCartney always wrote quickly and easily, taking ideas where he found them. For example, *Let It Be*:

> "I had a dream one night about my mother. She died when I was fourteen so I hadn't really heard from her in quite a while. It gave me some strength. *'In my darkest hour, mother Mary comes to me'*."

The house, being so close to the studios, became a regular meeting place and stop-over for the other Beatles during recording sessions.

**Adam Ant's** mother worked as a cleaner for McCartney in the late 1960s and her son attended Marylebone Grammar School before entering the music world.

**4** | Where: 52 Hamilton Terrace
Who: **TREVOR HORN-ZTT RECORDS**
When: 1990s

Home of leading producer, Trevor Horn.

Horn has produced Frankie Goes To Hollywood and, amongst others, the recent work of Tom Jones. He is joint owner of ZTT records and has played in several groups, including The Art Of Noise, Yes and Buggles.

**Seal** recorded *Crazy* at Horn's studios at 60 Beethoven Street, in West Kilburn.

**5** | Where: Primrose Hill
When: 1960s-1990s

**THE ROLLING STONES** were photographed for the cover of *Between The Buttons* on Primrose Hill in November 1966 after an all-night recording session. Gered Mankowitz took the photo, fuzzy around the edges, mirroring their physical state at the time. The album was released in January 1967.

Also...

The park was also where **PAUL McCARTNEY** used to walk his Old English Sheepdog, Martha.

And...

**MADNESS** had their photo taken here in 1982, for the album, *The Rise & Fall*.

Lead singer, Suggs, born Graham McPherson, went to Quinton Kynaston School, nearby on Marlborough Hill in the 1970s.

And...

**OASIS** used the park as the backdrop for the cover of their 1995 single, *Wonderwall*.

**22 Hill Road** home of Liam Gallagher and Patsy Kensit in 1996

**6** | Where: 22 Hill Road
Who: **LIAM GALLAGHER-OASIS**
When: 1996

Liam Gallagher retreated here after leaving the band on their 1996 US tour.

The house belonged to his girlfriend, Patsy Kensit. She had bought it with ex-husband, Jim Kerr of Simple Minds. The house has been sold and the couple moved to 132 Loudoun Road in St John's Wood.

Gallagher blamed the stresses of house-hunting as the reason for quitting the Oasis tour at Heathrow airport. Others blamed his up-and-down relationship with brother Noel.

**7** | Where: 18 Hill Road
Who: **CHRISSIE HYNDE**
When: 1996

This house is owned by Chrissie Hynde of The Pretenders. She moved to Hill Road some time after divorcing Jim Kerr of Simple Minds and now lives here with her daughter from her relationship with Ray Davies of The Kinks.

**18 Hill Road** home of Chrissie Hynde

**132 Loudon Road** rented home of Liam and Patsy in 1996

**8** | Where: 132 Loudoun Road
Who: **LIAM GALLAGHER-OASIS**
When: Autumn 1996

Liam Gallagher and Patsy Kensit's £2,000 a week rented house, where they lived whilst searching for somewhere to buy.

**9** | Where: Elgin Avenue
Who: **BJORK**
When: 1996

Icelandic star, Bjork, lives here and can often be seen in the local shops with her son, Sindri.

**8 St John's Wood Terrace** home of Noel Gallagher in 1996

**10** | Where: St John's Wood Terrace
Who: **OASIS**
When: 1996-present

Oasis songwriter, Noel Gallagher lived and worked at no.8 during the success of *(What's The Story) Morning Glory*.

His brother Liam bought no.14 in Spring 1997 with Patsy Kensit soon after they married.

## Camden NW1

**1** | Where: 1A Camden Road, The Camden Palace
Who: **THE POLICE**
When: 28 May 1977

Andy Summers, Sting and Stewart Copeland first played together here as Strontium 90.

Ex-Curved Air guitarist Summers replaced Henry Padovani, officially in June when the group renamed themselves The Police.

**2** | Where: 5 Kentish Town Road, Holts Footwear
Who: **MADNESS**
When: 1979

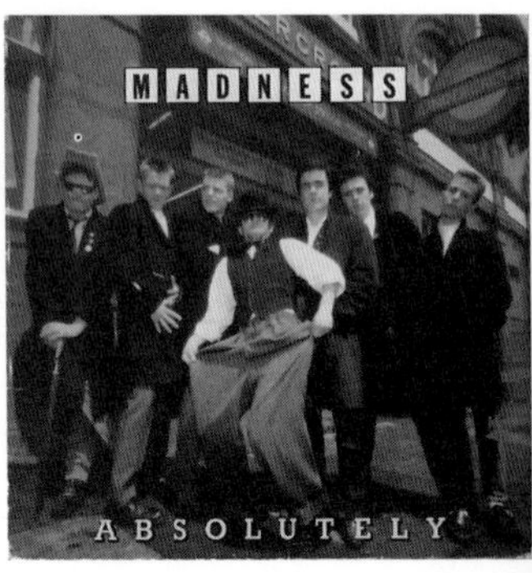


In their first years together, Madness rehearsed in a room above the shoe shop. They often played at the Dublin Castle Pub at 94 Parkway.

Many Madness album covers have been taken in the area: e.g. the cover for *Absolutely* was taken outside Chalk Farm tube station.

**3** | Where: 184 Camden High Street, Electric Ballroom
Who: **SID VICIOUS**
When: 22 August 1978

Sid Vicious last performed here before leaving for the US. The concert was called 'Sid Sods Off' and Glen Matlock, another ex-Sex Pistol, was a member of his band. Sid Vicious, named after his hamster and his violent behaviour, had replaced Matlock in The Pistols.

Vicious was born John Beverley and went to Hackney and Stoke Newington College of Further Education. He died in New York of a heroin overdose, having been charged with the murder of his girlfriend Nancy Spungen.

**4** | Where: 208 Camden High Street, Tilley's Restaurant
Who: **THE EURYTHMICS**
When: 1971

Annie Lennox worked in this café when she arrived in London in 1971 and had quit the Royal Academy of Music.

The Eurythmics later rehearsed and recorded above a picture framers down the road, for their debut album *Sweet Dreams*. It sold over a million copies.

**5** | Where: Camden Market, off Camden High Street
Who: **FINE YOUNG CANNIBALS**
When: 1984

Roland Gift was working on a stall here when he was asked by ex-Beat members Andy Cox and David Steele to join Fine Young Cannibals as lead singer. By December they had released *Johnny Come Home,* their first hit.

**6** | Where: 100 Chalk Farm Road, The Roundhouse
When: 1960s

**PINK FLOYD** played at the launch party for the International Times (IT) underground magazine which took place during Easter 1966, supported by Soft Machine. This was also the opening night of the Roundhouse as a concert venue. Previously it had been a warehouse for Gilby's Gin.

Pink Floyd headlined due to the popularity of their light show. They also played two benefit concerts for IT at Alexandra Palace in summer 1967. At the second, their lead singer Syd Barrett's drug-taking first became a problem when he was unable to function on stage.

Also...

**ELTON JOHN** performed at a music festival in summer 1968 and by accident kicked over his piano stool. The reaction of the audience led him to make it a permanent part of his act.

And...

**LED ZEPPELIN** played under their new name for the first time on 9 November 1968, having changed from The New Yardbirds. The gig was on the same day that Robert Plant married his pregnant girlfriend.

And...

**DAVID BOWIE** performed solo here for the first time in February 1970. Tony Visconti, Mick Ronson and John Cambridge made up his band. Ronson continued working with Bowie in The Spiders from Mars and Visconti produced.

**7** | Where: Chalk Farm Road, Chalk Farm Railway Yard
Who: **THE CLASH**
When: 1976-1978

'he Clash used the Atlanta Rehearsal Rooms for about three years.

On 13 August 1976 they played their first live gig at the railway yard to a small udience. The photo for the back cover of their debut album *The Clash* was aken here early the next year, 1977.

On 30 March 1978, Mick Jones and Paul Simonon were arrested when a police elicopter caught them shooting at pigeons from the roof of the building. They vere fined £800.

**8** | Where: Albert Street
Who: **NOEL GALLAGHER-OASIS**
When: 1990s

asis songwriter Noel Gallagher lived in Albert Street when the group first oved down to London from Manchester. The road was conveniently close to asis's record company, Creation Records, at 109 Regent's Park Road.

# Hampstead & Belsize Park NW3

**1** | Where: 42a Hampstead High Street
Who: **THE SEX PISTOLS**
When: 1975

John Lydon lived in this squat. There was no running water and this, along with the state of his teeth, led to his nick-name, Johnny Rotten. Here he started to write lyrics for future Sex Pistols' songs.

Sid Vicious, recalling the squat, said that rival punk-group, The Clash, only wrote songs about the dole, "cause of me and Rotten moaning about living in a poxy squat in Hampstead. It was them coming up there and seeing the squalor we were living in that encouraged them to write."

**2** | Where: 10a Holly Hill
Who: **THE ROLLING STONES**
When: July 1964-Spring 1965

Keith Richards and Mick Jagger moved to the ground floor flat here after their first tour of the US in June 1964.

**18 Well Road** home of Boy George

**Foley House** on East Heath Road

**3** | Where: 18 Well Road
Who: **BOY GEORGE**
When: 1990s

oy George moved here after Culture Club had brought him financial success nd when he was pursuing a solo career. It was also from here, that George was rested during his heroin addiction.

**4** | Where: 11 East Heath Road, Foley House
Who: **NICK MASON-PINK FLOYD**
When: 1990s

ome to Nick Mason, drummer with Pink Floyd.

Though originally a four-piece group, Pink Floyd is now officially only Dave lmour and Nick Mason, after lyricist Roger Waters left and keyboardist Rick right became a salaried employee. The massively successful Pink Floyd tours are derwritten by Mason and Gilmour: they also receive the lion's share of the ns of millions profit. Mason's share is worth £38 million. Gilmour is worth £55 llion and Roger Waters £35 million.

**5** | Where: 108 Frognal
Who: **STING**
When: 1980s

STING'S OLD HOME AT **108 FROGNAL**

Sting lived here in the early years of his solo career before moving to Highgate:

"My songs are like a diary where you can look back after ten years and say what my preoccupations were."

Sting is now worth £55 million.

**6** | Where: Oakhill Park, off Frognal, 'Weeping Ash'
Who: **GEORGE MICHAEL**
When: 1990s

In this exclusive road, George Michael lives in a modern house which drops down the hill from the road. Apart from the privacy, Michael likes the proximity to the heath where he walks his dogs.

During his long lay-off from recording caused by a legal battle with his record

**WEEPING ASH** GEORGE MICHAEL'S HOME IN OAKHILL PARK

company, Sony Music, Michael became almost a recluse here, spending his time writing for what became his 'comeback' album, *Older*.

Michael's company, Dreamworks, paid Sony £40 million to release him from the disputed contract. This reduced his personal wealth to £45 million.

**Decca Studios** in Broadhurst Gardens



**7** | Where: 165 Broadhurst Gardens, Decca Studios
When: 1960s

**'HE BEATLES** had their notorious failed audition for Decca Records at ›roadhurst Gardens on 1 January 1962.

It was cold and they were tired and nervous after the long trip from Liverpool. onsequently the group did not perform at their best, with Paul McCartney's ɔice freezing up.

Decca had space to take on only one group and the decision was made by Dick ɔwe to take on **Brian Poole and the Tremeloes**, believing their sound more ɔmmercial.

However, the tapes of the Beatles' audition led to a deal with EMI.

Within a year, Decca's Dick Rowe became the laughing stock of the industry as 'he man who turned down The Beatles".

Ironically, it was through George Harrison's recommendation that Rowe's ɔutation was saved a year later when he signed a new group: **The Rolling ones**.

so…

**AVID BOWIE** auditioned for Decca here in September 1966 and recorded me of his early songs, including *The Laughing Gnome*. Decca subsequently ned him on their label, Deram.

d…

**FLEETWOOD MAC's** Mick Fleetwood, John McVie and Peter Green, raided the studios one night to make a demo that would become their first album.

Raided could be an exaggeration. Stories have varied. Some say that John Mayall offered them studio time. As they were in John Mayall's band, the Bluesbreakers, at this time, it is possible.

John Mayall soon fired Peter Green and Mick Fleetwood, enabling them to set up on their own as Fleetwood Mac.

The new band rehearsed at the Black Bull pub on the Fulham Road in preparation for their debut at the Windsor Jazz and Blues Festival in August 1967.

**8** | Where: Mapesbury Road, Kilburn
Who: **THE ROLLING STONES**
When: 1963-July 1964

With some money reaching them from the success of their first hit *Come On*, manager Andrew Oldham moved The Stones from the squalor of Edith Grove into the relative cleanliness of a flat on Mapesbury road.

It was here that Mick Jagger and Keith Richards began to write songs. As Richards described it:

> "Andrew Oldham locked Mick and myself into a kitchen in this horrible little apartment. He said, 'you ain't coming out' and there was no way out. We were in the kitchen with some food and a couple of guitars, but we couldn't get to the john, so we had to come out with a song."

**9** | Where: 169-171 High Road, Willesden Green, Morgan Studios
When: Spring 1970

**PAUL McCARTNEY** recorded sessions here for his first solo album *McCartney* in Spring 1970.

The album, completed at his Scottish home-studio on the Isle of Mull, was released at the same time as *Let It Be* on 23 May 1970, much to the annoyance of the other Beatles. *McCartney* rose to No.1 in the US charts and No.2 in the UK.

When visiting the studio, McCartney used the name 'Billy Martin' to keep the others in the dark as to what he was doing. The fact that he was making a rival record to The Beatles was a cause of much bitterness between Lennon and McCartney.

Also...

**THE KINKS** recorded the album *Lola Vs Powerman And The Money-Go-Round Part One* here in 1970. 'Part Two' never appeared. The sessions at the studio were intended only as demos, but they ended up on the album.

The album included the song *Lola* about two people, one a transvestite, who meet at a night-club. *Lola* reflects the sexual ambiguity of its songwriter, Ray Davies, at the time.

**10** | Where: 6 Wychcombe Studios, off England's Lane
Who: **DAVE STEWART & SIOBHAN FAHEY**
When: 1990s

Dave Stewart, ex-Eurythmics, lives with wife Siobhan Fahey, ex-Bananarama an currently with Shakespeare's Sister, in this wooden-fronted house.

**Wychcombe Studios** belonging to Dave Stewart

**11** | Where: 9 Steele's Road, 'Supernova Heights'
Who: **NOEL GALLAGHER-OASIS**
When: 1997 onwards

Noel Gallagher, reputedly a millionaire forty times over, lives here with Meg Mathews, now his wife, after moving from St John's Wood Terrace. He bought the house in 1996 for a million pounds and spent many months renovating it before moving in the beginning of 1997.

Noel and Meg married in Las Vegas on 7 June 1997 at the Little Church of the West. They also own a country house in Chalfont St Giles in Buckinghamshire.

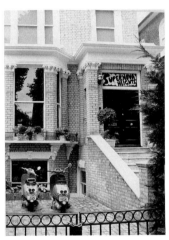

**Supernova Heights** home of Noel Gallagher

**12** | Where: Chetwynd Road
Who: **MADNESS**
When: Late 1970s

Madness regard the Camden area as their home: most members of the band went to Gospel Oak School in Mansfield Road.

The group formed in 1977 as The Invaders and early rehearsals were held at the home of Mike Barson, the keyboardist, on Chetwynd Road.

# Islington N1

**1** | Where: 35 Britannia Row, Britannia Row Recording Studio
Who: **PINK FLOYD**
When: 1971-1990s

This converted chapel was made into a recording studio and offices by the group. Pink Floyd originally bought the building to store equipment between tours.

They recorded *Animals* here in 1976 and the first demos for *The Wall*.

Twenty-three pupils from the fourth form of Islington Green School sang with Dave Gilmour on *Another Brick In The Wall (Part Two)* for the album. A real teacher from the school, Alan Redshaw, was the voice of 'the teacher'. The school's contribution took only half an hour to record. It was Pink Floyd's first single hit since *Arnold Layne* in 1968.

*The Wall* was made into a film in 1981, starring Bob Geldof. Locations included The New Horticultural Halls in Victoria and the disused Beckton Gasworks in the Docklands. The Tilbury Skinheads played the Nazi Hammer Guards.

Roger Waters bought a house nearby and converted the garden tool shed into his own studio.

**2** | Where: 83 Upper Street, The Screen on the Green
Who: **THE CLASH**
When: 29 August 1976

The Clash played their first gig at a punk festival here. They had formed in June and rehearsed in disused railway sheds nearby in Chalk Farm.

**3** | Where: 207 Upper Street, The Hope & Anchor
When: 1970s & 1980s

**U2** played their first London gig here to nine people in December 1979. They had come over from Dublin to look for a record deal.
Also…
**JOY DIVISION** in December 1978 and **DEXY'S MIDNIGHT RUNNERS** in June 1979 also made their London debuts here.
Also...
**FRANKIE GOES TO HOLLYWOOD** filmed the promotional videos for *Relax* and *Two Tribes* in the basement of this pub in October 1982.

**4** | Where: 8 Compton Terrace
Who: **MADNESS**
When: June 1977

Madness played their first gig at a party in this house, opposite The Hope & Anchor. At this time, they were called The Invaders and Suggs (Graham McPherson) was yet to join as vocalist.

**5** | Where: 70 Barnsbury Road, Anna Scher Children's Theatre
Who: **SPANDAU BALLET**
When: Late 1960s

Martin and Gary Kemp of Spandau Ballet learnt their acting skills at this youth theatre.

They attended the drama school until they were fifteen years old and went on to star together in the British film, 'The Krays'.

Most of the members of Spandau Ballet went to the Dame Alice Owen School in Owen Street, EC1.

**6** | Where: Caledonian Road, Pentonville Prison
Who: **THE STRANGLERS**
When: January-April 1980

Lead singer, Hugh Cornwell, served a three month sentence for possession of heroin and cannabis.

Cornwell wrote the autobiographical book 'Inside Information' about his time there.

Two years later, The Stranglers had their biggest commercial success with a song about heroin, *Golden Brown*.

The group had been part of the punk scene of the late 70s when they seemed to always be in the centre of controversy: the sexism of the songs *Peaches* and *Nice 'N' Sleazy*; strippers on stage at a concert in Battersea Park and banned from performing by various councils.

**7** | Where: 29 Furlong Road
Who: **ELTON JOHN**
When: 1968

Elton John lived here in the basement flat with songwriter Bernie Taupin. Elton described how they wrote songs:

> "The first thing we wrote together was a thing called *Scarecrow*, then there was a song called *One Time, Sometime Or Never* which Spencer Davis was going to record. When we started, Bernie's lyrics would never be in verse form; there'd just be 115 lines and I'd say 'where the fuck do I start?'"

Elton's girlfriend Linda Woodrow soon moved in with them. They had met on Christmas Eve 1967 at the Cavendish Club in Sheffield.

The song, *Someone Saved My Life Last Night,* is about Elton's suicide attempt at the flat. He tried to gas himself when he was depressed, stressed and feeling trapped at the thought of marriage to Linda:

> "When I lived with her she used to beat me up. But we got this flat in Islington and for six months I was in love and idyllically happy. But … she hated my music and wanted to marry me. My mother and Bernie thought I was mad. But because it was the first relationship of my life I defended it and clung to it."

Afterwards, Elton John and Bernie Taupin moved back to Pinner for a while to stay with Elton's mother.

## Highgate N6

**1** | Where: Compton Avenue, 'Roundhill' (private road)
Who: **RINGO STARR-THE BEATLES**
When: Autumn 1969-September 1973

After selling 'Brookfield', his country mansion, Ringo Starr moved back to London. The Beatles split up and Starr recorded the albums *Sentimental Journey* and *Ringo* whilst living here.

He sold the house after his divorce from first wife, Maureen Cox.

Starr then bought Tittenhurst, John Lennon's old home, and lived there in the early 1970s.

**2** | Where: 21 Hampstead Lane
Who: **STOCK, AITKEN & WATERMAN**
When: 1996

Matthew Aitken, of Stock Aitken and Waterman, lives here.

They wrote and produced for many acts of the mid 1980s, including **Kylie Minogue**, **Jason Donovan** and **Danni Minogue**.

Michael Stock lives in Sidcup, Kent and Pete Waterman in Warrington, Cheshire.

**3** | Where: 2 & 4 The Grove
Who: **STING & ANNIE LENNOX**
When: 1990s

In this row of exclusive houses overlooking Hampstead Heath, Sting and Annie Lennox, both successful solo artists, are neighbours.

## Finchley N3

**1** | Where: 73 Church Lane, Neasden
Who: **GEORGE MICHAEL**
When: 1960s

George Michael grew up here as Georgios Kynacos Panayiotou. His Greek Cypriot father ran several businesses in the area, including a restaurant and a launderette.

**2** | Where: Kingsbury High School, Princes Avenue
When: 1950s-1970s

**THE ROLLING STONES'** drummer, Charlie Watts, went to school here in the 1950s.

And…

**GEORGE MICHAEL** came here for a few years before moving to Bushey in Hertfordshire in the early 1970s.

**3** | Where: St Paul's Church, Finchley
Who: **CLIFF RICHARD**
When: April 1967

Cliff Richard was christened at this church by the Bishop of Willesden.

Originally marketed as a 'bad boy', Cliff became a family entertainer during the mid 1960s. This coincided with his interest in Christianity after joining the American evangelist, Billy Graham, on stage at Earl's Court.

Cliff studied at Oakhill Theological College in nearby Oakwood and achieved an O' level in Divinity a couple of months before his christening.

## Finsbury Park N4

**1** | Where: Finsbury Park Tube Station
When: 1970s & 1980s

**GRAHAM BOND** was a pioneer of British Blues. Though he achieved limited commercial success with The Graham Bond Corporation, his influence was widespread amongst sixties' musicians from The Stones to Eric Clapton.

He committed suicide under a train at the tube station in May 1974 whilst depressed and suffering from drug addiction.

And...

**THE POGUES**' Shane McGowan and Jem Finer busked at the station before finding the various members of the Irish folk group at surrounding pubs in the early 1980s.

**2** | Where: 232-236 Seven Sisters Road, Rainbow Theatre
(formerly Finsbury Park Astoria)
When: 31 March 1967

**JIMI HENDRIX** first burnt his guitar on stage at the Rainbow on 31 March 1967.

The premeditated act was designed to upstage other performers: **The Walker Brothers** and **Cat Stevens**.

As he played *Wild Thing*, Hendrix's guitar caught fire. The management were not happy with the stunt. Although Hendrix received slight burns, the publicity ensured that it became a regular part of his act.

Also...

**PINK FLOYD** played the live premier of *Dark Side Of The Moon* here on 17 February 1972, a year before the album was released.

*Dark Side Of The Moon* established Pink Floyd's commercial success after the uncertainty of Syd Barrett's departure.

It was recorded at Abbey Road and engineered by Alan Parsons, later of The Alan Parsons Project. Revolutionary for its recording techniques and for madness as its subject, the album has sold over 20 million copies.

And...

**ERIC CLAPTON**'s comeback concert at the Rainbow on 13 January 1973 was arranged by Pete Townshend of The Who.

Since mid-1971, when he had played in Derek and The Dominos, Clapton had been a recluse at Hurtwood Edge in Surrey. During that time he was suffering from an addiction to heroin and had been inactive, except in 1972 when *Layla* came out. The song expressed his love for Patti Boyd, the wife of his best friend, George Harrison.

The concert was a success, although it started badly when Clapton failed to arrive on time and people feared he would not turn up. However he did, blaming his lateness on increased weight which meant his stage trousers had to be let out.

# Muswell Hill N10

**1** | Where: Creighton Avenue, William Grimshaw Grammar School (now Creighton Comprehensive)
When: 1950s

**THE KINKS**' leader Ray Davies, and his younger brother Dave, went to school here. Davies met Peter Quaife at the school and formed his first band, The Ray Davies Quartet.

Also…

**ROD STEWART** was a year below Ray Davies at the school. Stewart played a lot of football and was a prefect. He lived above his parents' newsagents shop at 507 Archway Road (now demolished).

Stewart had a summer job at Highgate Cemetery digging graves and when he left school, he tried-out for Brentford Football Club in west London.

**2** | Where: Fortis Green Road
When: 1950s

**THE KINKS**' Ray and Dave Davies lived in a house opposite the Chissold Arms pub during their childhood.

In the front room on the piano, Ray Davies thought up the song, *You Really Got Me*, with one of the most recognised and imitated riffs in pop music.

Many of The Kinks' songs were inspired by this North London area: the cover photographs for the 1971 album, *The Muswell Hillbillies*, were taken in the Archway Tavern, Archway Close.

Also…

**FAIRPORT CONVENTION** were named after the house on the corner with Fortismere Road.

Now a doctor's surgery, Fairport House was home to the folk-rock group's guitarist, Simon Nicols.

**3** | Where: Connaught Gardens
Who: **THE KINKS**
When: Mid 1960s

The band shared a flat here in the early years of their success.

Ray Davies spent most of the time perfecting his songs, whilst the others enjoyed their celebrity.

**4** | Where: Ellington Road
Who: **ROD STEWART**
When: 1969-1971

Rod Stewart lived in Ellington Road when he joined The Faces in June 1969.

Here, Stewart wrote for The Faces with Ron Wood, including *Stay With Me*. He also wrote *Maggie May* which launched his solo career. The song recalled Stewart's seduction by an older woman in 1962, during a CND protest at Aldermaston, Berkshire.

As his solo career took off, Stewart bought a house in Winchmore Hill before moving to Windsor.

**5** | Where: Hornsey College of Art, 77 Crouch End Hill
When: 1960s

**THE KINKS**' Ray Davies went to the college in the early-sixties, before going to Croydon Art School.

After seeing Alexis Korner perform at the college, Davies formed a blues group in which he played piano.

And...

**DEEP PURPLE**'s bass guitarist, Roger Glover, went to the same art college.

**6** | Where: 84-86 Tottenham Lane, Hornsey, Konk Studios
Who: **THE KINKS-RAY DAVIES**
When: May 1973 onwards

Ray Davies bought Konk Studios in 1973. It was here that, amongst other work, he developed The Kinks' concept albums of the seventies.

Davies was in the studio during the 1980 riots in Turnpike Lane, just around the corner, and wrote The Kinks' song, *Give People What They Want* whilst hearing the commotion outside.

The early seventies were stressful for Davies. In June, just after buying the studios, his wife left him, taking their two daughters. Davies took an overdose and was admitted to Highgate Hospital.

**7** | Where: Turnpike Lane Tube Station
Who: **SADE**
When: 1980s

Sade Anu lived near Turnpike Lane before she achieved success.

One day, unemployed and broke, she sheltered at the tube station during a rain storm and wrote the lyrics to *When Am I Going To Make A Living?*

**8** | Where: 147 Crouch Hill, Church Studios
Who: **THE EURYTHMICS**
When: 1980s

By the time their second album *Touch* was recorded in 1984, Dave Stewart and Annie Lennox owned this recording studio in a converted church.

Lennox wrote much of her early Eurythmic's work whilst living at 26 Warwick Avenue and uses her life as material for her songs:

> "I don't feel I am in control, actually - I think being a creative person is just being a vehicle, I just want to be a vehicle. ... A song like *Love Is A Stranger* is emotionally sadomasochistic. It's not the love act, nothing so literal, but it is taken from my experience. It's about falling for people who never want you and feeling ambivalent towards the people who do want you. I've hurt people and felt totally cold about them, but when it's happened to me, I can't take it. My best songs come from suffering because I've indulged in my pain..."

THE LIVE AID CONCERT AT **WEMBLEY STADIUM** IN 1985

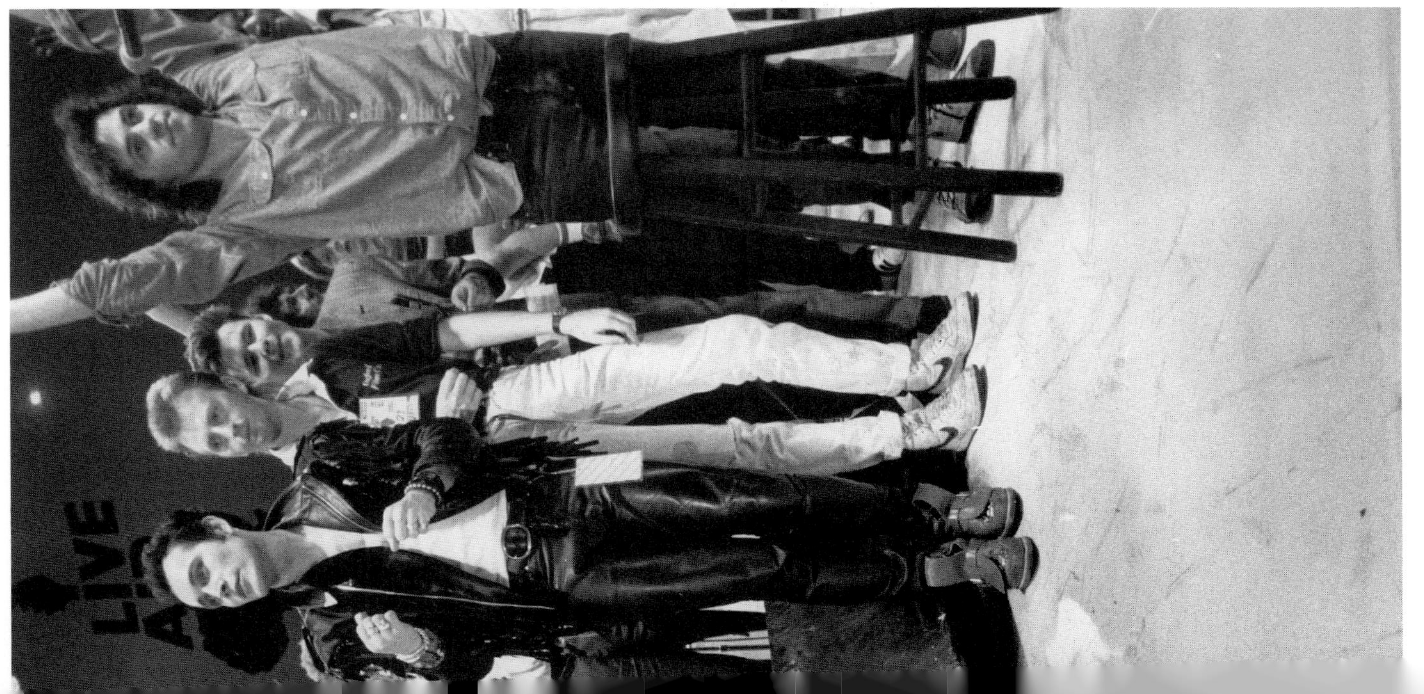
LIVE

# Totteridge N20 & Winchmore Hill N21

**Montebello** home of producer Mickie Most

**1** | Where: 19 Totteridge Common, 'Montebello'
Who: **MICKIE MOST**
When: 1980s onwards

Mickie Most, real name Michael Hayes, built this house for £4 million.

From the 1960s to the early 1990s, Most was one of the most consistently successful producers with over 400 million records sold.

The groups he has produced range from **The Animals**, **Herman's Hermits**, **The Yardbirds** and **Jeff Beck** to **Kim Wilde**.

**2** | Where: Percy Road, Winchmore Hill
Who: **CLIFF RICHARD**
When: April 1960 onwards

Cliff Richard bought a house here to live in with his family on the success of *Living Doll*.

Born in India as Harry Webb, Cliff soon came to England to live in Enfield. He went to Cheshunt Secondary Modern School in Windmill Lane.

He left school to work as a credit control clerk at Atlas Lamps (Ferguson's) on Great Cambridge Road. In the evenings he would go to the 2i's Coffee Bar in Soho, where he was discovered.

# Wood Green N22

**3** | Where: 287 High Road, Wood Green, The Fishmongers Arms
Who: **THE FACES-ROD STEWART**
When: 1969

The Faces often rehearsed at this pub. It was a popular venue for bands starting out, including Led Zeppelin and Fleetwood Mac.

# Wembley HA9 & Greenford UB6

**1** | Where: Empire Way, Wembley Empire Pools
Who: **THE BEATLES**
When: 1 May 1966

Wembley Empire Pools, now Wembley Arena, has been a leading London concert venue since the 1960s.

The Beatles played their last UK concert at the NME Poll Winners' Concert here in May 1966. The group's last public concert was at Candlewick Park in San Francisco at the end of their 1966 US tour on 29 August.

**2** | Where: 28 Wembley Park Drive, Rediffusion Studios
Who: **THE ROLLING STONES**
When: 11-12 December 1968

Studios for the live recording of the last series of 'Ready Steady Go'. Rediffusion moved here from central London in 1965.

Nearby 'The Rolling Stones Rock 'n' Roll Circus' was filmed, with amongst others The Who, John Lennon, Eric Clapton and Jethro Tull.

Intended to compete with The Beatles' 'Magical Mystery Tour', the film was only released in 1996. Part of the reason was the perceived lack of quality of The Rolling Stones' performance, after waiting fourteen hours to play at 1.00am.

It was The Stones' last performance with Brian Jones, who died seven months later.

HE **OLDFIELD HOTEL** IN GREENFORD WHERE KEITH MOON JOINED THE WHO

**3** | Where: Oldfield Lane, Greenford, Oldfield Hotel
Who: **THE WHO**
When: Early 1964

hilst playing a gig here, The Who were approached by a drunken Keith Moon, essed totally in orange. Moon jumped on stage mid-set, declaring that he uld do better than their drummer. The Who let him try and discovered that he uld. Consequently they offered Moon the job.

Moon came from Wembley. He lived his childhood years in Chaplin Road and went to Alperton Secondary School.

The band discovered 'feedback' at the Oldfield with their new Marshall amps. This electronic sound became their trademark. However, George Harrison was the first to record feedback on *I Feel Fine*.

## Harrow HA1 & Pinner HA5

**1** | Where: Harrow College of Art, High Street, Harrow
When: 1960s & 1970s

**THE ROLLING STONES'** drummer Charlie Watts studied Graphic Design at the college in 1961.

And...

**THE SEX PISTOLS'** manager, Malcolm McLaren, attended in 1963. He met Vivienne Westwood here and they became partners, establishing a boutique on the King's Road where The Pistols formed.

And...

**ADAM ANT**, then known as Stuart Goddard, studied here for a short time before going to Hornsey Art School.

**FROME COURT** IN PINNER HOME TO ELTON JOHN IN THE 1960s

**2** | Where: 30 Frome Court, Pinner Road, Pinner
Who: **ELTON JOHN**
When: 1962-1967

Elton John lived in a ground floor flat with his mother, Sheila Dwight, and her partner Fred Fairebutcher.

Bernie Taupin moved in with Elton John for eighteen months after they left Furlong Road, Islington.

Many of their early songs were written here. *Your Song*, their first chart hit, was written in fifteen minutes around the breakfast table.

Since then, Elton John has had at least one chart hit each year.

**3** | Where: 55 Pinner Hill Road, Pinner
Who: **ELTON JOHN**
When: 1950s

Elton John grew up here, as Reginald Dwight, before the family moved to 111 Potter Street.

He went to Pinner County Grammar School (now Heathfield Girls School) and in 1964 he began playing professionally at the Northwood Hills Hotel on Friday, Saturday and Sunday nights:

> "I was there a year, singing Jim Reeves and Cliff Richard songs - anything that was popular ... things like *Roll Out The Barrel* ...otherwise you'd get a pint of beer slung over you. ... Eventually... it was packed out every weekend. It was great training because I played on an old upright piano that was out of tune and there were a couple of times when I had to dive out of the window when really bad fights broke out."

Whilst still at school, he won a scholarship for weekend tutoring at the Royal Academy of Music.

**4** | Where: St Edmund's Roman Catholic Church, Pinner
Who: **ELTON JOHN**
When: 1961

In 1961, Elton John joined his first band, The Corvettes. They were a local group who played at the church scout hut for £2 a night. He describes joining the band:

> "I met this guy ... who played guitar. I was very fat and when I said I played the piano he laughed hopelessly. I showed him. I did my Jerry Lee Lewis bit and he stopped laughing. We got a band together and played in scout huts."

They reformed as Bluesology in 1962, turning professional three years later after an audition at the Kilburn State Cinema led to their first single *Come Back Baby*, written by John.

Elton John left Bluesology when they became 'Long' John Baldry's backing band in December 1966.

It was at this time that he changed his name from Reg Dwight to Elton John, inspired by John Baldry and Bluesology sax player, Elton Dean.

**5** | Where: West Lodge Primary School, West End Lane, Pinner
Who: **SIMON LE BON-DURAN DURAN**
When: Late 1960s

Simon Le Bon was born in nearby Bushey and grew up in Pinner. He went to this school and sang in the choir at Pinner Parish Church.

Le Bon was studying drama at Birmingham University when he joined Duran Duran.

## Bushey WD2 & Watford WD1

**1** | Where: Bushey Mead's School, Harcourt Road
Who: **WHAM!**
When: Late 1970s

George Michael met Andrew Ridgeley at this school where they formed their first band, The Executive. Michael said:

> "I hadn't known it at the time, but the turning point in my early days was meeting Andrew Ridgeley at secondary school. He'd looked good, got the girls and wanted to be famous. He changed my life."

Their first gig was at the school scout hut on 5 November 1979. It was not long before they began song-writing, including *Club Tropicana* and *Careless Whisper*. They left in 1980, when amongst casual jobs and ceaseless clubbing, they sought a career in music.

Michael worked for a short while at a restaurant as a DJ:

> "The very last night ... I played the demo of *Careless Whisper*. I knew it didn't matter if I got into trouble because I had already given in my notice ... They had never heard it before and the floor filled."

However *Careless Whisper* was not a meaningful song for Michael:

> "It disappoints me that you can write a lyric very flippantly - and not a particularly good lyric - and it can mean so much to so many people. That's disillusioning for a writer."

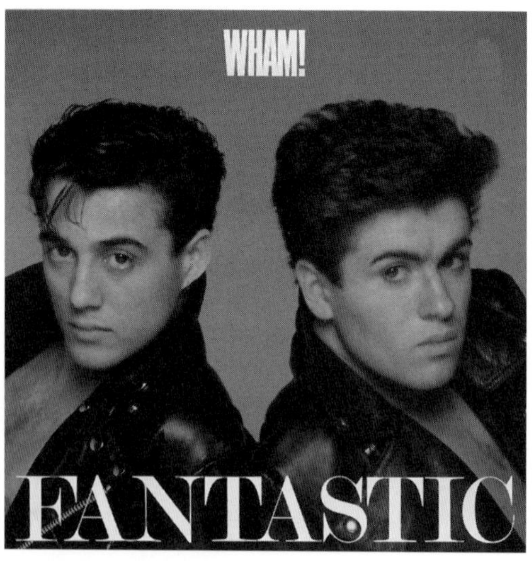


**2** | Where: 25 Chiltern Avenue, Bushey
Who: **WHAM!**
When: Late 1970s-1980s

This was the family home of Andrew Ridgeley. Amongst many of the songs the duo wrote here was *Last Christmas* and they used a tape recorder to make basic demos. George Michael had been given the tape recorder many years before:

**25 Chiltern Avenue** CHILDHOOD HOME OF ANDREW RIDGELEY

> "The first sign of my obsession with music was with an old wind-up gramophone that Mum had thrown out into the garage ... later they bought me a cassette with a microphone that I used to tape things from the radio - and then I became even more obsessive."

**3** | Where: Three Crowns Pub, Bushey
Who: **WHAM!**
When: 1982

After leaving school, George Michael was told by his father to make a success of music within six months or work for the family restaurant.

So, when Andrew Ridgeley met an executive of CBS Records at this pub, they were prepared to sign anything.

Thus, in March 1982, after rehearsing at the Hallingan Band Centre in Holloway, Michael and Ridgeley accepted a contract. Though this led to success within months with *Wham Rap*, it turned out to be financially disastrous for them. A disaster which was only rectified after a long and bitter court battle.

**4** | Where: Watford Football Club, Watford
Who: **ELTON JOHN**
When: 1970s onwards

It was from his childhood in Pinner that John grew to love Watford Football Club. In 1974 he bought the club and saw it rise through the divisions to become runner up of the Premier League:

> "I've been a Watford supporter ever since I was a kid living in Northwood. I used to get a Met line tube to Watford, walk up through the town and stand at the Rookery End. ... I used to stand up on the terraces to see them. Once I was beaten up by some fans of the opposing team. And now I'm on the board."

During the pressures of his early success and the stresses on his private life, John attributed his sanity to his affection for the club: "I was forced to take on responsibilities which forced me to have self-confidence for the first time. All I had been getting before was gold albums." John still regularly attends home matches, often bringing star guests with him to the directors' box.

## South-west London

# Fulham SW6

**1** | Where: 136 New King's Road, A&M Offices
Who: **THE POLICE**
When: 22 March 1978

Miles Copeland, manager of The Police, thought up the name of the band's first album *Outlandos D'Amour* sitting in a taxi outside the offices of A&M. He had just signed the band to A&M records.

The debut album was released in November and reached the UK top ten. Their last non-compilation album *Synchronicity* sold eleven million copies in five months when released in 1983. The Police recorded and produced their first two albums, *Outlandos* and *Regatta de Blanc* at the Surrey Sound Studios at 70 Kingston Road, Leatherhead in Surrey.

**2** | Where: 17 Wyfold Road, Marcus Recording Studio
Who: **TAKE THAT**

Take That, the Manchester group of five vocalists, recorded the single *Pray* at this studio. It was their first No.1 in the UK. Take That, the most successful boys-only dancing pop group, split in 1996.

**The Kings Head Pub** site of rehearsals for Unledded

**3** | Where: 4 Fulham High Street, Kings Head Pub
Who: **JIMMY PAGE & ROBERT PLANT**
When: 1994-1995

Jimmy Page and Robert Plant rehearsed for *Unledded* (for MTV) in a room above the pub.

Their reunion led to much speculation that Led Zeppelin were reforming. But though they did perform their earlier songs, they preferred to remain more low-key as a duo using a wider selection of musical influences, including fifty traditional Egyptian musicians.

# Battersea SW8 & Brixton SW2

**Battersea Power Station**

1 | Where: Battersea Power Station
Who: **PINK FLOYD**
When: 2 December 1976

'he power station is a favourite film location having been used for scenes from 'Help!', 'Quadrophenia' and countless promotional videos.

Its most famous use was by Pink Floyd for the cover of *Animals*. At the launch f the album, a giant inflatable pig was suspended over the power station. It nfortunately broke its anchor and floated free, causing havoc to aeroplanes vhich were instructed to "avoid the area due to a flying pig".

**Ramport Studios** in Thessaly Road

**2** | Where: 115-117 Thessaly Road, Ramport Studios
Who: **THE WHO**
When: 1970s

The Who converted this church building near Battersea Power Station into their recording studios.

They recorded *Quadrophenia*, their second rock opera, here using state-of-the-art quadraphonic equipment. The character, Jimmy, had four sides to his personality, each side represented by one member of The Who.

The cover for their 1974 album *Odds And Sods* was photographed here.

**3** | Where: Jebb Avenue, Brixton Prison
Who: **MICK JAGGER-THE ROLLING STONES**
When: 29 June 1967

Mick Jagger spent one night of a three month sentence for possession of four Benzedrine tablets. Released on bail the following day, the sentence was later quashed.

He had been arrested during a drug raid on Keith Richards' Sussex home, Redlands, on 12 February 1967. Jagger had already spent one night in Lewes jail after his trial in Chichester. Keith Richards spent the night at Wormwood Scrubs in West London, where Brian Jones was also to stay on a drugs charge later that year.

Jagger spent the night in Brixton writing the lyrics for *We Love You*, a thank you to fans for their support during the trials.

**4** | Where: Electric Avenue, Brixton
Who: **EDDY GRANT**
When: 1983

The Brixton riots of 1983 inspired Guyana singer Eddy Grant to write the hit song, *Electric Avenue*.

Educated in North London at Acland Burghley School, Grant played trumpet in the Camden Schools' Orchestra.

In 1973, he bought the Coach House Studios at 81 Osbaldestone Road in Stoke Newington, after years as a record producer and singing in the band, The Equals.

**5** | Where: 40 Stansfield Road, Brixton
Who: **DAVID BOWIE**
When: Late 1940s

Born David Jones, Bowie spent his first years here before moving to Bromley. He went to nearby Stockwell Infants School on Stockwell Road.

**0 STANSFIELD ROAD** THE CHILDHOOD HOME OF DAVID BOWIE

# Putney SW15 & Barnes SW13

**1** | Where: Pulman Gardens, Elliott School
Who: **PETER GREEN-FLEETWOOD MAC**
When: 1950s

Peter Green was born Peter Greenbaum in East London. The family moved to Putney and Green went to this school.

He began playing guitar in his early teens before joining John Mayall's Bluesbreakers, regularly appearing at the Pontiac Club at 200 Upper Richmond Road.

Green wrote Fleetwood Mac's early hits, including *Albatross, Oh Well* and *Man Of The World*, and left the group when he suffered from mental illness.

**2** | Where: Hotham Road, St Mary's Ballroom
Who: **THE WHO**
When: Early 1963

The Who supported The Rolling Stones at a gig here. Whilst watching them, Pete Townshend was impressed by Keith Richards' style of playing guitar, particularly his rotating arm when striking chords. Townshend copied him, making the 'Windmill' movement his own trademark.

**3** | Where: 3 Stag Lane
Who: **ELVIS COSTELLO**
When: Early 1970s

Elvis Costello lived here with his early band, Flip City, which he formed in 1971.

Costello went to Hounslow Secondary School before moving to Liverpool for a few years. On his return to London, he worked as a computer operator for the Elizabeth Arden Factory in Acton.

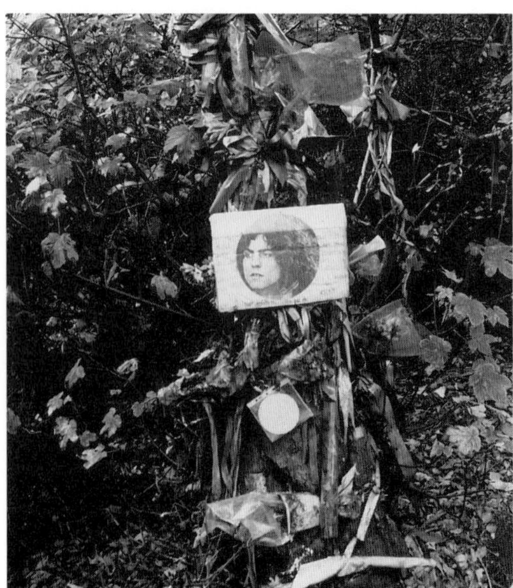

**QUEEN'S RIDE BRIDGE** WHERE MARC BOLAN DIED IN A CAR CRASH IN 1977

**4** | Where: Queen's Ride Bridge
Who: **MARC BOLAN**
When: 17 September 1977

Marc Bolan died instantly when his mini left the road and hit a tree on this bridge. The car was driven by girlfriend Gloria Jones.

They had been celebrating Bolan's forthcoming birthday at Morton's Club in Berkeley Square and were returning in the early morning to their home at 142 Upper Richmond Road. The bridge has been a memorial ever since.

**5** | Where: Ferry Lane
Who: **QUEEN**
When: April 1970

Brian May and Roger Taylor were living here when Freddie Mercury joined their band, Smile. Mercury suggested they change the name:

> "I thought up the name Queen … It's just a name, but it's very regal obviously, and it sounds splendid. … It had a lot of visual potential and was open to all sorts of interpretations. I was certainly aware of the gay connotations, but that was just one facet of it."

May came from Hampton and had gone to Hampton Grammar School. After leaving Imperial College he taught part-time at Stockwell Manor School. Mercury and Taylor had met working at Kensington Market.

The new band played their first gig for the College of Estate Management at Hornsey Town Hall in June 1971 when bassist John Deacon joined them.

**6** | Where: 117 Church Road, Olympic Studios
When: Mid 1960s onwards

**THE ROLLING STONES** recorded here during the sixties.

However, their first hit *Come On* was recorded at the Baker Street premises of Olympic in May 1963 before Decca moved the studios to Barnes in 1964.

Mick Jagger and Keith Richards began most of their songs in their home-studios before taking them to Olympic to develop with the rest of the group.

But *Jumpin' Jack Flash* began here at the studio when, in March 1968, Jagger and Richards arrived late for a rehearsal and heard Bill Wyman filling the time by experimenting with a riff on the piano. Richards was impressed and it became the basis of the song.

A year later, on 1 June 1969, Mick Taylor made his first recording with the group, *Honky Tonk Women*, replacing Brian Jones.

Taylor was replaced in 1975 by Ron Wood, from The Faces. Incidentally, Wood's elder brother ran the pub next door to the studios.

Also…

**ERIC CLAPTON** made his first recording when he played with **THE YARDBIRDS** in February 1964. Though previously they had made some demos at the R G Jones Studios in Wimbledon.

*For Your Love* was recorded here, in February 1965, and released just as Clapton left the band. It was The Yardbirds' breakthrough single. Clapton left, feeling the group were turning too much to pop and away from blues. *For Your Love* was written by Graham Gouldman, who was later part of the group 10CC.

**Olympic Studios** on Church Road in Barnes

And...

**TRAFFIC** recorded their first album *Mr Fantasy* in the summer of 1967 at the neighbouring studios to **THE SMALL FACES** who were recording *Itchycoo Park*.

Traffic lived in a cottage on the Fair Mile Estate, Aston Tirrold, Oxfordshire and wrote material for *Mr Fantasy*, which included *Hole In My Shoe* and *Paper Sun*.

And...

**THE TROGGS** recorded *Wild Thing* here in April 1966, their most successful release.

And...

**LED ZEPPELIN** recorded their first album at the studios in October 1968. It took only thirty hours over two weeks to complete.

They were called The New Yardbirds until Keith Moon of The Who suggested 'Lead Zeppelin', believing their music would sink them quicker than a zeppelin made of lead.

**7** | Where: Summertown, Wimbledon Stadium, Sun Cottages
Who: **MARC BOLAN-T REX**
When: 1950s & 1960s

Born Mark Feld at Hackney Hospital on 30 September 1947, Bolan lived with his parents at 23 Stoke Newington Common before moving here.

Bolan went to nearby Hill Croft School and left in his early teens to start a music career, recording under the name Toby Tyler.

It was at Sun Cottages that Bolan formed Tyrannosaurus Rex after placing an advert in a newspaper.

By 1971, his success allowed him to move to 47 Bilton Towers, Great Cumberland Place overlooking Regent's Park.

## Richmond TW9/10 & Twickenham TW1/2

**1** | Where: 184 Kew Road
Who: **PHIL LYNOTT**
When: 1980s

After the break up of Thin Lizzy, Phil Lynott had brief success as a solo artist. However his lifestyle became erratic due to insecurities and increasing use of drugs.

Lynott lived at this house with his wife Caroline until he died at Salisbury General Hospital in January 1986.

**2** | Where: 1 Kew Road, Crawdaddy Club (Bull & Bush)
Who: **THE ROLLING STONES**
When: Spring 1963

The Stones, recently joined by Charlie Watts on drums, played a Sunday night residency at this pub (then the Station Hotel) starting on 24 February 1963.

'The Richmond & Twickenham Times' began to report their gigs and on 14 April 1963 George Harrison of The Beatles attended a Sunday night session. Harrison was impressed and suggested to Dick Rowe of Decca that he sign them to the label.

The previous year Rowe had turned down the now successful Beatles and was keen to find the next big thing.

The success of The Stones' residency forced the Crawdaddy Club to move to the larger Richmond Athletic Club on 13 June 1963.

**3** | Where: South Western Hotel, opposite Richmond station (now Drummonds)
Who: **THE YARDBIRDS-ERIC CLAPTON**
When: October 1963

The 18 year old Eric Clapton auditioned for The Yardbirds one night as they rehearsed in this pub. His playing so impressed them that he was invited to join and was given the nick-name 'Slowhand'.

HE WICK ON RICHMOND HILL

**4** | Where: Richmond Hill, The Wick
Who: **RON WOOD-THE ROLLING STONES & THE FACES**
When: 1972-1996

Ron Wood bought this house, with one of the most spectacular views in south England, from actor John Mills in 1972, after his success with The Faces.

During a break in The Faces' schedule, Wood began work on a solo album *Got My Own Album To Do* and invited Keith Richards to contribute. Richards turned up late but ended up living in a house in the garden for four months. He was seeking refuge from police raids on his Cheyne Walk house.

Wood's friendship with Richards and his guitar style made him a perfect replacement in The Rolling Stones after Mick Taylor left in April 1975.

*It's Only Rock 'N' Roll* was recorded here in Wood's demo studio. Keith Richards says: "Mick originally cut this in Ronnie's house with David Bowie. We recut it later but kept the rhythm track from the original."

Pete Townshend bought the house in June 1996 for £2 million and began extensive renovations.

**Downe House** on Richmond Hill home of Mick Jagger

**5** | Where: 116 Richmond Hill, 'Downe House'
Who: **MICK JAGGER**
When: 1990s

Mick Jagger bought this double-fronted house as his London residence. It has magnificent views over the Thames. Jagger lives here with Jerry Hall and their three children. He bought the house for its privacy and for the ability to jog in peace around Richmond Park and the quiet residential streets. His parents live next door.

Jagger has an estimated wealth of £110 million. On The Rolling Stones' tour of 1995, the group played to over 4.5 million people around the world.

**6** | Where: Water Lane, Eel Pie Island Hotel
When: 1960s

The hotel, now demolished, was an influential jazz and blues club in the 1960s. Amongst the bands who played here were The Yardbirds, The Stones and The Who.

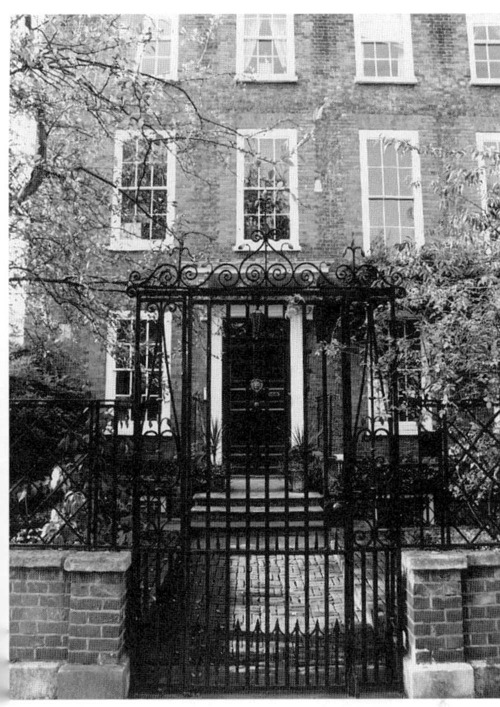

**TENNYSON HOUSE**
HOME OF PETE TOWNSHEND FOR MANY YEARS

**7** | Where: 15 Montpellier Row, Tennyson House
Who: **PETE TOWNSHEND-THE WHO**
When: 1980s-1996

Formerly home of the poet, Alfred Tennyson, it has been the home of Pete Townshend for many years. He has a recording studio in the next street, where he has written most of his recent work. His writing has become more reflective:

> "I feel that as a writer I haven't even started. If you are lucky to have a couple of hits they tend to weigh on you because they are born of innocence and honesty. Then you gather up experience and wisdom and cynicism, and it becomes much harder to use catch phrases and rhetoric to blame everyone else for what's wrong with the world or your life, and song-writing then becomes more complicated."

His wife still uses the house, despite Pete acquiring other properties in the area.

**8** | Where: The Barons, Twickenham Film Studios
Who: **THE BEATLES**
When: Early Spring 1964 & 2-15 January 1969

These film studios were used for most of the scenes in 'A Hard Day's Night', 'Help!' and 'Let It Be'.

The surrounding area was used for location shots, for example, Aisla Avenue for the opening scene in 'Help!'. Each Beatle was filmed getting out of a Rolls Royce and entering separate houses that, inside, became one.

Other locations around London for The Beatles's promotional films include:

- Angel Lane, Stratford E16: used as Liverpool for *Penny Lane* and *Strawberry Fields* for BBC's 'Top of the Pops' in February 1967.
- Chiswick House, Burlington Lane W4: used on 20 May 1966 for *Paperback Writer* and *Rain*.
- Knole Park, Sevenoaks, Kent: the grounds were used for *Penny Lane* and *Strawberry Fields*.

  During filming, John Lennon visited an antiques shop in Sevenoaks and saw a poster advertising 'Mr Kite and His Circus' playing at Bishopsgate. Lennon wrote the song *Being for the Benefit of Mr Kite* taking many of the lyrics directly from the poster.
- West Malling Airfield, near Maidstone, Kent: used for *Magical Mystery Tour* and *I Am the Walrus* during 19-24 September 1967.

**9** | Where: Ranelagh Drive, The Boathouse
Who: **PETE TOWNSHEND-THE WHO**
When: 1976 onwards

Pete Townshend bought this riverside property in 1976 and converted it into a studio where he worked on the late Who and his early solo albums.

Townshend's Eel Pie Recording Productions Ltd was based at the Boathouse.

**78 CONSTANCE ROAD** CHILDHOOD HOME OF PHIL COLLINS

**10** | Where: 78 Constance Road, Twickenham
Who: **PHIL COLLINS**
When: 1950s

Born at Chiswick Maternity Hospital (along with members of The Who and Deep Purple), Phil Collins lived here for most of his childhood.

He went to Chiswick County Grammar School, Burlington Lane.

**11** | Where: 453 Hanworth Road, Hounslow
Who: **PHIL COLLINS-GENESIS**
When: 1970s

After he joined Genesis as drummer in the early 1970s, Phil Collins moved to this house with his mother. He remained here when Peter Gabriel had left the group and he became vocalist.

## West London

# Hammersmith W6/12

**1** | Where: Crisp Road, Riverside Studios
Who: **THE SEX PISTOLS**
When: 1975

Early rehearsal rooms for Glen Matlock, Steve Jones, Paul Cook and Wally Nightingale, before John Lydon joined the band.

Malcolm McLaren, living with his grandmother in Thurleigh Court, Balham, sacked Nightingale and named them The Sex Pistols. By the time Lydon joined, The Pistols were rehearsing in Wandsworth at the Rose & Crown Pub on the High Street.

**2** | Where: 157 Hammersmith Road, The Red Cow Pub
When: 1970s

**AC/DC** made their first UK appearance at this pub in April 1976. They had recently arrived from Australia and were living in Lonsdale Road in Barnes.
Also...

**STING** played his first London gig at this venue in January 1977, when still in the Newcastle band, Last Exit. He had just given up a career in teaching to come down to London to try music.
And...

**THE JAM** were given a residency in January 1977 at the Red Cow, shortly after their first set of London gigs at the 100 Club, Oxford Street and the Greyhound on Fulham Palace Road.

**3** | Where: Lime Grove, Hammersmith College Of Art
When: Mid 1960s-1970s

**CAT STEVENS** was studying here in 1966 when he was discovered by producer Mike Hurst. Hurst secured him a contract with Decca's new label, Deram. He soon released *I Love My Dog*.

*Matthew And Son* was the next single and a bigger hit, reaching No.2 in the UK. He later made his version of *Morning Has Broken* and wrote *Wild World*.
Also...

**THE CLASH's** Mick Jones studied here in the mid-1970s. He worked for the Post Office and formed The Clash in June 1976 when he lived in a squat near Shepherd's Bush Green. Jones had previously played in the punk band, London SS.

**4** | Where: 150 Goldhawk Road, Townhouse Studios
When: Late 1970s-1980s

**THE JAM** recorded their album *Setting Son* at the studios in October 1979. Many of the songs for the album, including *Eton Rifles*, were written in the studio during the recording sessions.

Also...

**PETER GABRIEL** in 1979 recorded the first sessions for *Games Without Frontiers*, the song that launched his solo career. It became his first hit after leaving Genesis over four years before, in May 1975.

And...

**FREDDIE MERCURY** recorded *Barcelona* at the studios in 1987.

Freddie Mercury sang a duet with Spanish opera star, Monserrat Caballé, on the album which saw the coming together of his operatic aspirations, an interest that was manifest in Queen's *Bohemian Rhapsody* in 1975.

**5** | Where: 339 Goldhawk Road, Queen Charlotte's Hospital
Who: **JOHN LENNON-THE BEATLES**
When: December 1968

Yoko Ono stayed here when she miscarried due to the pressures of her court appearance for drugs.

John Lennon and Ono recorded tracks for *Unfinished Music No 2 - Life With The Lions*, at her bedside.

All Ringo Starr's children were born here, including Zak, now drummer with The Who. (Zak Starkey was taught to play drums by Keith Moon.)

THE WHO PERFORMING AT THE SHEPHERD'S BUSH BINGO HALL IN THE 1960S

**6** | Where: 15 Percy Road
Who: **ROGER DALTRY-THE WHO**
When: 1950s

Born at Hammersmith Hospital, Roger Daltry lived here during his teens.

**7** | Where: 22 St Peters Square, Island Records
Who: **BOB MARLEY**
When: Late 1970s

Island Records moved to Hammersmith in the late 1970s. Chris Blackwell, Island's owner, was born in Jamaica and his interest in Jamaican reggae brought Bob Marley to the label. Blackwell went to Harrow School in North-west London and is worth £110 million.

When in England, Marley lived around the corner from the Island offices, in a house in British Grove and played football with his band, The Wailers, in Battersea Park, SW11.

**8** | Where: Chiswick Mall
Who: **THE SMALL FACES**
When: 1968

Steve Marriott moved to this riverside road when The Small Faces became successful.

He wrote *Lazy Sunday Afternoons* for neighbours who complained about his noise.

## Acton W3/4

**1** | Where: 205 Goldhawk Road, Social Club
Who: **THE WHO**
When: Early 1960s

Roger Daltry played here with his first bands after leaving school and working at the local steel yard.

The Who played at the club during their first months together, along with gigs at the White Hart Hotel at 264 High Street, Acton.

**2** | Where: 20 Beaumont Road, Eden Studios
Who: **ELVIS COSTELLO**
When: Late 1978

Elvis Costello recorded *Oliver's Army* here, his first big hit:

> "I was using yesterday's records as blueprints, as all pop music is. All the good pop clichés had been written and there hadn't been any new ones for a while. I wanted to take some ready-made clichés … and come up with my photo-negative versions of them. Almost every song on my first album was an opposite - a diseased version of another song."

**3** | Where: East Acton Lane, Barbara Speake Stage School
Who: **PHIL COLLINS**

Phil Collins went to drama school here; it led him to parts in the crowd scene of The Beatles' film 'A Hard Day's Night' and the stage musical 'Oliver'.

4 | Where: 13 Second Avenue
Who: **DEEP PURPLE**
When: October 1968

The original line-up of Deep Purple lived here before their first tour of the US in October 1968.

Six months later, Roger Glover and Ian Gillan joined.

5 | Where: Gunnersbury Lane, Acton County Grammar School
Who: **THE WHO**
When: Late 1950s-1961

The three members of The Who attended school here, Roger Daltry being one year ahead of John Entwistle and Pete Townshend.

Townshend's father played professionally in a swing band and Entwistle was a member of the Middlesex County Youth Orchestra.

Whilst at school, Townshend and Entwistle formed a skiffle band, The Confederates. Daltry was expelled in 1960 for refusing to wear his school uniform. He asked Entwistle, and then Townshend, to join his group, The Detours, in 1962.

Ian Gillan singer with Deep Purple also attended school here.

## Ealing W5

1 | Where: 42A The Broadway, The Ealing Club
Who: **ALEXIS KORNER**
When: 1961

Alexis Korner was instrumental in the spread of 'blues' in England. He ran The Ealing Club, where many bands played, including his own Blues Incorporated.

The club saw many future big names pass through including John Entwistle, Charlie Watts, Brian Jones, Paul Jones and Mick Jagger, all of whom played with and were helped by Korner.

Korner gave **Free** their name after seeing them play in 1968 at the now defunct Blue Horizon Club at 205 York Road in Battersea. Within two years, Free had hit the big-time with *All Right Now*.

2 | Where: 35 Sunnyside Road
Who: **PETE TOWNSHEND-THE WHO**
When: 1961-62

Pete Townshend often stayed at the ground floor flat of American college friend, Tom Wright. When Wright was deported back to the US because of his drug use, Townshend took over the flat and his large collection of rhythm and blues records.

Townshend spent his nights performing with Entwistle and Daltry, getting up early to attend college whilst the others slept on in the flat.

Along with his first experimentation with drugs and art, Townshend began to write songs seriously, though he felt none were yet good enough to perform.

Amongst the many visitors to Townshend's flat was Andy Newman, an eccentric post office engineer and a musician who introduced him to jazz and the then novel form of multi-track recording.

**20 Woodgrange Avenue**

In 1969, Townshend produced *Something In the Air* which became a No.1 for Andy 'Thunderclap' Newman.

Towards the end of his time at Sunnyside Road, The Who turned professional.

**3** | Where: 20 Woodgrange Avenue
Who: **PETE TOWNSHEND-THE WHO**
When: 1963-64

Pete Townshend lived on the top floor of his parents' house when he left art school.

Townshend tried to make a studio by soundproofing the floor with concrete until his parents kicked him out when their ceiling began to cave in.

**4** | Where: St Mary's Road, Ealing College of Art and Technology
When: 1960s

**RON WOOD** of The Faces and The Rolling Stones came to the college in the early 1960s.

And…

**THE WHO**'s Pete Townshend went to the College in 1961, where he became fascinated by theories of self-destructive art. This resurfaced in The Who smashing their equipment on stage and trying to capture pure noise in their music.

[Townshend was taught by Robert Brownjohn who later designed the cover to The Rolling Stones' album, *Let It Bleed*.]

At college, Townshend began performing with Daltry and Entwistle. The pressures eventually forced Townshend to make a choice between college and music. Townshend asked the Head of the Graphics Department for advice: when told how much the group was earning, the teacher advised him to grab his chance and leave immediately.

And…

**FREDDIE MERCURY** studied graphic art and design at the college in the late 1960s. Born Frederick Bulsara in Zanzibar, Tanzania, Mercury moved with his family to nearby Feltham. He was lead singer in several groups before joining Queen in 1970.

## Kennington SE11 & Elephant & Castle SE1

**1** | Where: Cleaver Square
Who: **TIM FINN-CROWDED HOUSE & SPLIT ENZ**
When: Mid-1980s

New Zealander Tim Finn lived here with actress Greta Scaachi when launching his solo career. He wrote the Crowded House songs *Four Seasons In One Day* and *Weather With You* for Scaachi whilst here.

**2** | Where: Kennington Oval, Oval Mansions
Who: **IAN DURY**
When: 1978

Ian Dury lived in a bedsit on the 5th floor overlooking the cricket ground, whilst writing the early Blockheads' lyrics. The council flats were dirty and run-down and Dury referred to them as "the cat-shit mansions".

**3** | Where: 490 Old Kent Road, Workhouse Studios
When: Late 1970s onwards

**IAN DURY & THE BLOCKHEADS** recorded the album *New Boots And Panties* here in early 1978.
Also...
**PAUL YOUNG** recorded his first solo album *No Parlez* at the studios in late 1982, which went on to sell over seven million copies.

## Greenwich SE10 & Eltham SE9

**1** | Where: 65-67 Greenwich High Road, White Swan Pub
Who: **DIRE STRAITS**
When: Summer 1977

Mark Knopfler came across a jazz group at this pub playing their regular weekly session. He described them in the group's first single *Sultans Of Swing*.

The demo was made at Pathway Studios, 2A Grosvenor Avenue in Islington and after the tapes were played on Radio London, Dire Straits were offered a recording contract with Phonogram.

**2** | Where: 138 Deptford Church Street, Farrar House
Who: **DIRE STRAITS**
When: Spring 1977

Former journalist, Mark Knopfler, moved into his brother David's ground floor flat here and started to take his song writing seriously:

> "People who create things, even things which you think, 'God, that's great' and then you see that the guy is irresponsible, you see that the guy isn't committed to what he's doing, doesn't stay with it, has other people turn it out for him; you realise as you get older that art without responsibility is bull-shit."

The first gig that the band played was in July 1977 at a party outside the back of the flats. They played their first public concert under the name Dire Straits at the Albany Theatre as the support to **Squeeze**, another Deptford band.

Knopfler, as the main songwriter, is now worth £65 million.

**3** | Where: 29 Joan Crescent, Eltham
Who: **BOY GEORGE**
When: 1960s & early 1970s

Boy George, real name George O'Dowd, spent his childhood at the family home here. He went to the local Eltham Green School, leaving for Central London in September 1975 after he was expelled.

**4** | Where: Goldsmiths College, Lewisham Way, New Cross
When: 1960s onwards

**THE SEX PISTOLS**' manager, Malcolm McLaren came to the art department of the college in 1968 for three years.

And…

**DIRE STRAITS**' bass guitarist, John Illsey, studied sociology here before joining the group in 1977.

And…

**THE VELVET UNDERGROUND**'s only British born member, John Cale, studied here before going to New York on a Leonard Bernstein scholarship.

And…

**BLUR** formed when Alex James and Graham Coxon were at the college.

## Bromley BR1/2 & Beckenham BR3

**1** | Where: Bromley Registry Office
Who: **DAVID BOWIE**
When: 20 March 1970

David Bowie married Angela Barnet here. They married so that Angie, an American, could remain in Britain.

A few days before the wedding, *The Prettiest Star*, which he wrote for her, was released.

**2** | Where: 4 Plaistow Grove, Sundridge Park
Who: **DAVID BOWIE**
When: 1955-1965

David Bowie lived here for ten years with his parents after previous homes at 23 Clarence Road and 106 Canon Road in Bromley. His father, Hayward Jones, worked for Dr Barnados children's homes.

On his fifteenth birthday, Bowie was given a book on the sax player Gerry Mulligan by his elder half-brother, Terry Burns. This started Bowie's interest in music and thoughts of a career as a performer. He bought a saxophone and began playing jazz.

Like their mother and three aunts, Burns suffered from mental illness. He was eventually moved in 1969 to the high security hospital, Cane Hill, outside Croydon. Bowie visited him several times at the hospital. Burns committed suicide at Coulsdon South railway station in 1985.

**4 Plaistow Grove** home to David Bowie during his school years

The 'family illness' has been influential in Bowie's music. His brother, in particular, inspired *All The Madmen* on *The Man Who Sold the World* and *The Bewlay Brothers* on *Hunky Dory*.

**3** | Where: Bromley Technical High School, Oakley Road
Who: **DAVID BOWIE**
When: 1958-1963

After going to Burnt Ash Junior School in Rangefield Road, David Bowie, then David Jones, went to Bromley Technical School (now Ravenswood School). At the school, Bowie damaged his eye in a fight over a girl. This left him with mismatched eyes: one brown, one green.

And...

One of his teachers was the father of **PETER FRAMPTON**, who further inspired Bowie when he played the guitar at school concerts. Frampton left in 1966 at sixteen to join The Herd and later Humble Pie, before releasing in 1976 *Frampton Comes Alive!*, the biggest-selling live album ever.

Frampton joined Bowie as lead guitarist on his 1987 'Glass Spider' Tour.

**4** | Where: High Street, Beckenham, The Rat & Parrot Pub
Who: **DAVID BOWIE**
When: Spring 1969

Bowie, now living back in Beckenham at 24 Foxgrove Road, set up the Beckenham Arts Lab, above this pub, then the Three Tuns.

Set up in 1969 as a performance space, it culminated with the Beckenham Free Festival about which Bowie wrote *Memory Of A Free Festival*.

**5** | Where: 42 Southend Road, Haddon Hall (demolished)
Who: **DAVID BOWIE**
When: November 1969-1972

David Bowie moved here after the success of *Space Oddity*.

The ground floor flat, with its gothic atmosphere, became the meeting place for a wide circle of friends and musicians. Most of the *Hunky Dory* and *Ziggy Stardust* albums were written at this time. Whilst living here, Bowie's son was born, inspiring the song *Kooks*. The cover photograph for *Hunky Dory* was taken in the garden.

**6** I Where: 38 Miall Walk, Lower Sydenham
Who: **BILL WYMAN-THE ROLLING STONES**
When: 1936 - 1940s

Bill Wyman, born William Perks, lived in Beckenham and went to Beckenham & Penge Grammar School for Boys in Penge. He still lived in the area with his wife when he joined The Stones in 1962.

**THE RAT & PARROT PUB** SCENE OF BOWIE'S ARTS LAB IN 1969

## Dartford DA1|2|3|4

**1** I Where: 33 Chastillian Road
Who: **KEITH RICHARDS**
When: Late 1940s-1950s

Keith Richards spent the first years of his life here, before the family moved to the new council estate at Temple Hill. His mother worked at a cake shop on the High Street and his father worked as a foreman at the Osram factory in Hammersmith.

**2** I Where: 39 Denver Road
Who: **MICK JAGGER**
When: 26 July 1943-1950s

Mick Jagger's childhood home, close to Keith Richards at Chastillian Road.
Jagger's father was a fitness instructor, who instilled in him a daily regime of physical exercise in the back garden, much to the amusement of Jagger's neighbourhood friends.

**3** I Where: James Road, Wentworth Primary School
Who: **MICK JAGGER & KEITH RICHARDS**

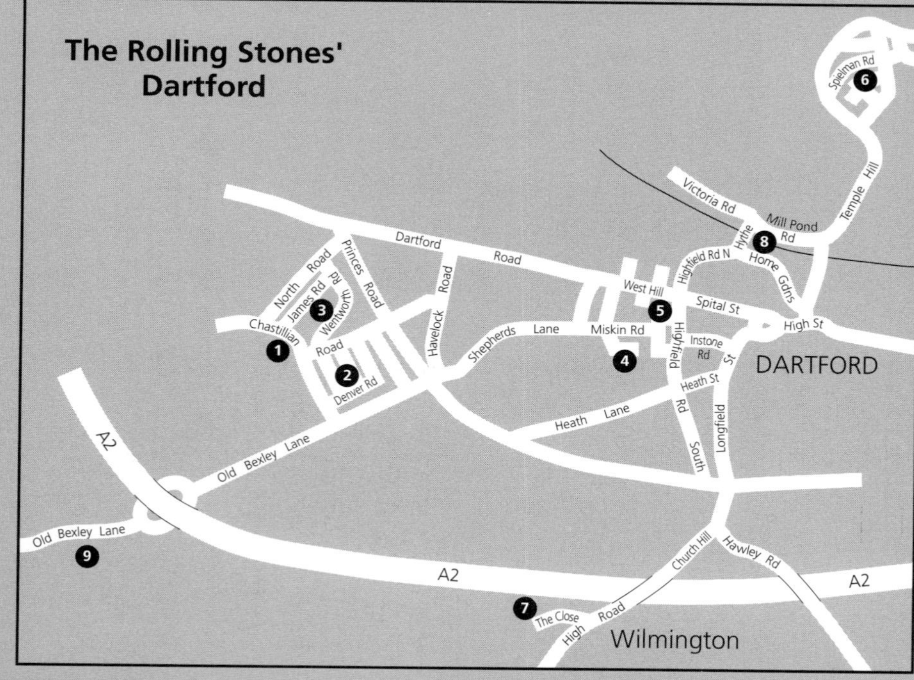

The Rolling Stones'
Dartford
Dartford Road
North Road
James Rd
Wentworth Rd
Princes Road
Chastillian Road
Denver Rd
Havelock Road
Shepherds Lane
Miskin Rd
West Hill
Highfield Rd N
Victoria Rd
Mill Pond Rd
Hythe
Home Gdns
Temple Hill
Spielman Rd
Spital St
High St
Highfield Rd
Instone Rd
Heath St
Heath Lane
South Rd
Longfield St
DARTFORD
Old Bexley Lane
A2
Church Hill
Hawley Rd
The Close
High Road
Wilmington
1
2
3
4
5
6
7
8
9

**39 Denver Road**

**6 Speilman Road**

When: Early 1950s

Jagger and Richards first met as young children at this school.

**4** | Where: Miskin Road, Dartford Technical School
Who: **KEITH RICHARDS**
When: Late 1950s

After leaving Wentworth Primary School, Richards came here.

His voice was good enough to join the school choir and he sung soprano in a Christmas concert of Handel's *Messiah* for the Queen at Westminster Abbey and at inter-school competitions:

> "Only three of us used to be good enough to do the hallelujahs. I was a star then - coming up to London to sing at the Albert Hall. I think that was my first taste of show business. When my voice broke they didn't want me in the choir any more. Suddenly it was 'don't call us, we'll call you'. I think that was when I stopped being a good boy and started being a yob."

**5** | Where: West Hill, Dartford Grammar School
Who: **MICK JAGGER**
When: Late 1950s

Mike, as Jagger was known, was a keen sports player and an enthusiastic pupil, leaving the school with seven O' levels, two A' levels in English and History and an entry to the London School of Economics.

At school with him was Dick Taylor (later of **The Pretty Things** ) with whom Mick formed the group Little Boy Blue and the Blue Boys. They played songs by Chuck Berry and Little Richard and any other American blues artist whose records they could get their hands on.

**6** | Where: 6 Spielman Road, Temple Hill
Who: **KEITH RICHARDS**

When: 1954-1962

Keith Richards and his family moved here in 1954 from their previous home at Chastillian Road.

His mother bought Richards his first guitar and the lonely child spent his time trying to copy skiffle and rock 'n' roll hits.

Richards is today worth £80 million.

**7** | Where: The Close, Wilmington, 'Newlands'
Who: **MICK JAGGER**
When: Late 1950s

The Jagger family moved to a larger house in Wilmington, causing Mick Jagger to lose touch with his neighbour, Keith Richards.

**8** | Where: Home Gardens, Dartford Train Station
Who: **KEITH RICHARDS & MICK JAGGER**
When: 1960

Mick Jagger and Keith Richards re-met in their late teens on the London-bound platform.

Jagger was going to lectures at the LSE and Richards to Sidcup Art College where he was studying Technical Illustration.

Also at Sidcup were Phil May, founder of **The Pretty Things**, and Dick Taylor one of the original Stones, who had been at school with Jagger. Richards did not attend many lectures at college, visiting only to collect his grant cheque and to play his guitar in the lavatories (where the acoustics were good).

At the train station when they re-met, Jagger had a collection of records with him and their friendship was revived when they discovered their common passion for blues music. Richards then joined Dick Taylor and Jagger in Little Boy Blues & The Blue Boys.

**9** | Where: Old Bexley Lane, Bexley Hospital
Who: **MICK JAGGER**
When: Late 1950s & 1970s

Here in a cupboard, Mick Jagger lost his virginity to a nurse when working during a school holiday at the hospital.

Coincidentally, his ex-girlfriend, **Marianne Faithfull**, spent seven months at Bexley Hospital in the seventies trying to cure her drug addiction.

## East London

# Plaistow E13 & East Ham E6

**1** | Where: 23 Barking Road, Plaistow, The Bridge House Hotel
Who: **DEPECHE MODE**
When: November 1980

It was whilst playing a gig at this music venue, that Depeche Mode were seen and offered a contract by Mute Records. Their first hit single *Just Can't Get Enough* appeared in August 1981.

Vince Clark, Andy Fletcher and Martin Gore formed the group in 1980, all three having known each other at St Nicholas School in Basildon, Essex. Dave Gahan, the vocalist, joined later in the year and they played their first gig together at St Nicholas.

Another 1980s group, Blancmange, were discovered at The Bridge House.

**2** | Where: 445-57 High Street North, East Ham
Who: **THE SMALL FACES**
When: 1965

It was whilst working at the J60 Music Bar here, that Steve Marriott met Ronnie Lane to form The Small Faces with Kenny Jones.

## Stratford E15

**1** | Where: 157 Chobham Road, The Eagle
Who: **DAVID ESSEX**
When: 1964

David Essex was discovered playing drums for a group here by Derek Bowman of 'The Daily Express', who later became his manager. He released his first solo single in April 1965 but did not achieve commercial success until 1973 with *Rock On,* although his acting career did take off, when he played Jesus in 'Godspell' in 1971.

**2** | Where: 27 The Broadway, The Two Pudding Pub
Who: **THE THE-MATT JOHNSON**
When: 1950s

Matt Johnson, of The The, grew up above this pub which was run by his father and renowned for live music.

## Forest Gate E7 & Manor Park E12

**1** | Where: Woodgrange Road, Forest Gate, The Upper Cut
Who: **JIMI HENDRIX**
When: 26 December 1966

The Jimi Hendrix Experience played a gig at The Upper Cut disco on Boxing Day.

Whilst waiting to go on stage, Hendrix sat in the dressing room and wrote *Purple Haze*. During that performance, it was played for the first time.

**2** | Where: 26 Strone Road, Manor Park
Who: **STEVE MARRIOTT-THE SMALL FACES**
When: 1950s

Steve Marriott, lead singer with The Small Faces, grew up here.

As a teenager, Marriott frequented nearby Manor Park Cemetery. It was known in the area by courting couples as 'Itchy Park', because of the stinging nettles. *Itchycoo Park* was the single that broke them into the US in 1967.

## Outside London

# Surrey

**Kenwood** home of John Lennon in the 1960s

**1** | Where: Weybridge, Wood Lane, 'Kenwood'
Who: **JOHN LENNON**
When: July 1964-10 November 1968

John Lennon moved to Kenwood when Beatlemania made it impossible for him to live in London.

Lennon turned the house into a private fantasy world of gadgets and curiosities. His increasing discomfort with public adulation led him to more contemplative songs, for example *Nowhere Man* (autumn 1965). Nearly all the major songs of Lennon's middle Beatle period were written at Kenwood, often during the night with the flickering of the television screen for background.

Lennon described writing *Help!* in early 1965:

> "I was actually crying out for help. It was my 'fat Elvis' period. I was very insecure and completely lost, and I am singing about when I was so much younger, looking back at how easy it was."

In early 1967, during work on the *Sergeant Pepper* album, he was inspired when his son Julian returned from Heath House School in Portmore Road, Weybridge, with a drawing. It was of a class-mate, Lucy O'Donnell, and he told Lennon it was called 'Lucy in the sky with diamonds'.

*Across the Universe* was written one spring morning in 1968 when he woke up at Kenwood with the words *"pools of sorrow, waves of joy"* in his head.

Despite his success, Lennon said that he was disillusioned until he met Yoko Ono:

"Here I am, rich and famous as I always wanted to be, and nothing's happening."

Of Weybridge, he said:

> "It won't do at all. I'm just stopping here like a bus stop. Bankers and stockbrokers live here. I think of it everyday. Me in my Hanzel and Gretal house. I will take my time. I will get my real house when I know what I want. You see there is something else I'm going to do. Something I must do. Only I don't know what it is. That's why I go round painting and taping and drawing and writing and that. Because it may be one of them. All I know is this isn't it for me."

In 1968 Lennon's wife, Cynthia, returned from a holiday in Greece to find her husband with Yoko Ono and her marriage over.

Paul McCartney described writing *Hey Jude*:

> "I happened to be driving out to see Cynthia at Kenwood. I think it was just after John and she had broken up, and I was quite mates with Julian [their son]. … And I was going out in my car just vaguely singing this song, and it was like, 'Hey Jules' … and then I thought a better name was Jude. A bit more country and western for me."

Amongst the many publicity photographs taken at Kenwood was the cover for *Rubber Soul,* taken in the garden.

**2** | Where: Weybridge, South Road, 'Sunnyheights'
Who: **RINGO STARR**
When: 1965-1969

Ringo Starr lived just down the road from Lennon.

Here Starr wrote *Octopus's Garden* about the pond in the grounds, for the *Abbey Road* album.

He sold the house in 1969 to Stephen Stills of Crosby, Stills and Nash, moving to Peter Sellers' old house, Brookfields, Cot Mill Lane, Elstead.

Starr is today worth about £55 million. Some of his personal wealth comes from the voice-overs for 'Thomas the Tank Engine'.

**3** | Where: Weybridge, St George's Hill, 'Torpoint'
Who: **TOM JONES**
When: 1966-1975

After the success of *It's Not Unusual*, Tom Jones moved to this exclusive residential development.

Gordon Mills, his manager, lived nearby. In the early 1970s, Mills' new signing, **Gilbert O'Sullivan**, lived in a cottage at the bottom of his garden for several years. O'Sullivan wrote *Clair* for Mills's daughter whom he often baby-sat.

O'Sullivan left Mills in 1979 after a court battle for unpaid royalties, though Jones stayed with Mills until his death in the 1980s.

**4** | Where: Esher, 16 Claremont Drive, 'Kinfauns'
Who: **GEORGE HARRISON**
When: July 1964-1969

George Harrison lived in this bungalow during the height of The Beatles' success.

Here, Harrison developed his many interests from Eastern spirituality to the sitar.

Harrison was taught the instrument by Ravi Shankar, whom he had met in 1965 at a friend's house in Fitzalan Road, north London.

*Revolver* was the first album to feature his playing, with original demos recorded at Kinfauns in early 1966. The effect was revolutionary, with songs like *Love You To* which blended translated Buddhist lyrics with the eerie sound of the sitar.

Harrison married Patti Boyd at Esher Registry Office on 21 January 1966.

They met during the filming of 'A Hard Day's Night' when Boyd, at the height of her modelling career, had a part.

Harrison wrote *Something* for her. It is his most successful song, having been recorded by countless artists and played in excess of seven million times on radio around the world.

**5** | Where: Ripley, 'Hurtwood Edge'
Who: **ERIC CLAPTON**
When: 1969-1991

Eric Clapton bought this nineteenth century Arab-style mansion in 1969, with the earnings from the recently disbanded Cream.

Born Eric Clapp, he grew up in the area and lived with his grandparents at No.1 The Green, after the marriage of his parents broke-up. He went to the village primary school and St Bede's Secondary Modern School.

From 1961-62, Clapton went to Kingston College of Art to study stained-glass design before leaving to join The Yardbirds.

*Here Comes The Sun* was written by George Harrison in Clapton's garden during the summer of 1969, when Harrison sought escape from the endless business affairs of the breaking-up Beatles.

Clapton and Harrison wrote extensively together, including *My Guitar Gently Weeps* and *Badge*, and remained close friends even when Harrison's wife, Patti Boyd, left to live with, and eventually marry, Clapton.

During the 1970s Clapton's addictive personality led him into heroin and alcohol abuse and he spent years living as a recluse at Hurtwood Edge.

However, two of his greatest songs were written during this period, and both inspired by Boyd: *Layla* about his longing for her, and *Wonderful Tonight* reflecting the peace he felt with her. (*Wonderful Tonight* was written after attending the first Buddy Holly Convention, organised by Paul McCartney in September 1976.)

Clapton sold the house in 1991 after the death of his son Connor and moved to Chelsea. The four-year old was buried in the churchyard at Ripley, after falling out from a window in New York. Clapton wrote the song *Tears In Heaven* in his memory. Clapton is today worth about £60 million.

**6** | Where: Forest Green, The Parrot Inn
Who: **PROCOL HARUM-GARY BROOKER**
When: 1980s

Gary Brooker, the co-writer of Procol Harum's *A Whiter Shade Of Pale*, owned The Parrot Inn during the 1980s.

Eric Clapton, living nearby, played occasionally at the pub and joined Brooker on his solo album *Lead Me To The Water*. In the late 1980s, Brooker joined Clapton's band.

**7** | Where: Epsom, Miles Road
Who: **JIMMY PAGE-LED ZEPPELIN**
When: 1950s

Jimmy Page grew up here at his parents' house. After going to Sutton Art School, Page began session work in London and played guitar for, amongst others, The Who on *I Can't Explain*, Lulu on *Shout*, Them on *Here Comes The Night* and Dave Berry on *The Crying Game*. He spoke of how his extensive session work led to problems:

> "I didn't really do that much on Kinks records. ... I know that Ray [Davies] didn't approve of my presence. The Kinks just didn't want me around when they were recording. ... One aspect of being in the studio while potential hits were being made was the press - too many writers were making a big fuss about the use of session men."

His success as a session player led him to be invited to play in The Yardbirds with his childhood friend **Jeff Beck** (who had been to Wimbledon Art School).

**8** | Where: Woking, Stanley Road
Who: **PAUL WELLER**
When: 1950s-1960s

Paul Weller lived in his family home here for much of his youth.

Weller began to play guitar at Sheerwater Comprehensive School in Woking with Rick Buckler. Later they were joined by Bruce Foxton to complete The Jam line-up. When Weller's father, a former boxer, offered to manage them, they turned professional.

Whilst living here, Weller wrote the early Jam songs. His childhood is remembered on his 1995 solo album, *Stanley Road*.

## Sussex

**9** | Where: West Wittering, Redlands Lane, 'Redlands'
Who: **KEITH RICHARDS-THE ROLLING STONES**
When: Mid-1960s

Keith Richards bought this moated medieval house in the mid-1960s. Despite being burnt down twice, Redlands remained Richards' home until the 1980s.

Before he bought his house in Cheyne Walk, Richard lived here, staying with Brian Jones at Courtfield Road when in London. Much of The Stones' mid-1960s music was written at the house.

In February 1967, Redlands was raided by the police leading to the prosecution of Richards and Mick Jagger for drug possession. Their minor infringement of pills caused an enormous uproar with tabloid descriptions of orgies, Satanism and Marianne Faithfull found naked with a Mars bar.

At their trial, they were sentenced to six months in prison which led to the famous 'Times' editorial "Who Breaks A Butterfly On A Wheel?" claiming the law was too heavily enforced in their case.

**10** I Where: Hartfield, Cotchford Farm
Who: **BRIAN JONES-THE ROLLING STONES**
When: November 1968-July 1969

Brian Jones moved to Cotchford Farm in November 1968 to try to regain his health. He had been suffering for several years from asthma, drug abuse and psychiatric problems. And his work with The Stones had become increasingly erratic.

In late spring 1969, Mick Jagger and Keith Richards drove to Cotchford Farm to inform Jones that he was no longer a member of the group, though he would be paid a future percentage of their earnings.

It came as a relief to Jones who had become disillusioned with the music The Stones were playing and wanted to return to a stronger blues sound.

Jones planned to form a new group and Cotchford Farm was renovated. He took great pride in owning this property where the 'Winnie the Pooh' books had been written.

On the night of 3 July, Jones tragically died when swimming in his pool. He was buried in the cemetery at Cheltenham, his birthplace.

**11** I Where: Peasmarsh, near Rye
Who: **PAUL McCARTNEY**
When: 1970s onwards

Paul McCartney owns a large estate outside Peasmarsh, part of which he farms. He lives here in a modest circular bungalow that he designed himself.

McCartney is worth £450 million. Some of his wealth comes from the one billion Beatles' records sold; the rest is from his solo work and music publishing business.

In the mid-1990s all three remaining Beatles met here to work on the *Free As A Bird* demo left by John Lennon.

**12** I Where: Loxwood, north of Billingshurst
Who: **PHIL COLLINS**
When: 1980s onwards

Phil Collins bought a mansion here, on the B2133, after the success of Genesis. He wrote material for his solo album, *No Jacket Required*, at the house.

Collins, with an estimated wealth of £120 million, is now a tax exile living in Switzerland with his girlfriend. He separated from his second wife, Jill, in the early 1990s.

At the end of 1996, it was speculated that Liam Gallagher of Oasis was interested in purchasing the property.

WOODSIDE HOME TO ELTON JOHN

**13** | Where: Old Windsor, Crimp Hill, 'Woodside'
Who: **ELTON JOHN**
When: Early 1976 onwards

ton John moved to Woodside after selling his bungalow 'Hercules' on the /entworth Estate in Virginia Water.

Hercules was his first out-of-London home, bought in 1972 after the success of ocket Man. He wrote the further hits *Crocodile Rock* and *Daniel* at the ungalow. Both were on the album *Don't Shoot Me I'm Only The Piano Player*. *rocodile Rock* was his first No.1.

'Woodside' is near to the Union Inn, just outside Windsor Great Park. His andmother lived in a bungalow in the grounds of the house until her death.

Whilst living in Windsor, Elton also owned homes in Holland Park and Chelsea rbour in central London. Today he is worth £150 million. His songwriter rtner, Bernie Taupin, is worth £45 million.

**14** | Where: Windsor Great Park, Cranbourne Court
Who: **ROD STEWART**
When: 1972-1975

Autumn 1972, Rod Stewart bought the 14 acre estate, Cranbourne Court, just side the Great Park.

le sold the property and moved to Los Angeles in 1975 when his group, The es, officially split.

**15** | Where: Ascot, London Road, Tittenhurst Park
Who: **JOHN LENNON**
When: August 1969-1972

n Lennon bought the eighteenth century mansion on 11 August 1969.

t Tittenhurst, he and Yoko Ono experimented with avant-garde music, nething he had not been able to do with The Beatles.

Much of his early solo work was written here, including *Imagine*, *Cold Turkey*, *Happy Christmas (War Is Over)* and *Instant Karma*.

The promotional film for the album *Imagine* was filmed around the house, as was the last photographic session of The Beatles as a group, used on the cover of the *Hey Jude* compilation album.

Within a couple of years of the break-up of The Beatles, Lennon moved to New York, feeling hemmed in and frustrated:

> "If I could be a fucking fisherman I would. If I had the capabilities of being something other than I am, I would. It's no fun being an artist. You know what it's like, writing, it's torture. I read about Van Gogh, Beethoven, any of these fuckers. If they had psychiatrists, we wouldn't have had Gaugin's great pictures."

Lennon sold Tittenhurst in 1972 to Ringo Starr, who lived here until the mid-1980s.

**16** | Where: The Thames at Pangbourne
Who: **JIMMY PAGE-LED ZEPPELIN**
When: 1960s

With the success of his session work, Jimmy Page moved from his parents' home in Epsom to a houseboat on the Thames here in 1965: "All my houses are isolated. Many is the time I just stay home alone. I spend a lot of time near water."

Page played in The Yardbirds. But after their break-up, he recruited Robert Plant and John Bonham from Birmingham and fellow session player John Paul Jones from Sidcup in Kent (who went to Christ's College School in Blackheath) to form The New Yardbirds.

Their first meeting together was at the houseboat where Plant outlined a tour of Scandinavia and plans for the future of the group.

It was during the tour that their name changed to Led Zeppelin, after Keith Moon's phrase for a bad group: "going down like a lead zeppelin".

**STARGROVES** COUNTRY HOME OF MICK JAGGER IN THE 1960S

**17** | Where: Near Newbury, 'Stargroves'
Who: **MICK JAGGER-THE ROLLING STONES**
When: 1960s & 1970s

In addition to various recording studios and their own mobile studio, The Stones used to record at Mick Jagger's country house, Stargroves.

Mick Jagger described recording *Bitch* at the house in 1971:

> "This is one of our groove tunes. We recorded the backing track at Olympic, but the overdubs, with the brass and everything, were done live one night in my house in the country, a sort of mock baronial hall I used to have called Stargroves, where The Who and Led Zeppelin also recorded later on."

## Oxfordshire

**18** | Where: Henley-on-Thames, 'Friar Park'
Who: **GEORGE HARRISON**
When: 1969 onwards

George Harrison bought this Victorian Gothic mansion in 1969, saving it from demolition.

After the break up of The Beatles, Harrison retired to Friar Park to write and record his multi-million selling *All Things Must Pass* triple album. He also revived the estate's seventy acres of magnificent gardens.

Harrison uses Friar Park for his many activities:

Dark Horse Records was set up in studios in the grounds, from where he writes his solo work.

Handmade Films has produced the Monty Python films, 'The Holy Grail' and 'The Life of Brian', and other British films including 'Mona Lisa' and 'The Long Good Friday'.

Harrison is worth £95 million, having lost £10 million on Handmade Films. His own songs account for about a fifth of his wealth, as The Beatles' catalogue of songs, worth over £300 million, gives each member of the group a share of about £75 million.

Harrison lives at Friar Park with his second wife Olivia Arras, whom he married in 1978, and their son Dhani.

## Essex

**19** | Where: Epping Forest, Copped Hall
Who: **ROD STEWART**
When: 1986 onwards

Rod Stewart bought this Elizabethan mansion on the edge of Epping Forest when he returned to England from Los Angeles. He still owns mansions in California and Florida.

Stewart is worth £60 million and in 1995 played live to an audience of 3.5 million in Rio de Janeiro.

The Beatles playing in **The Cavern** 1961

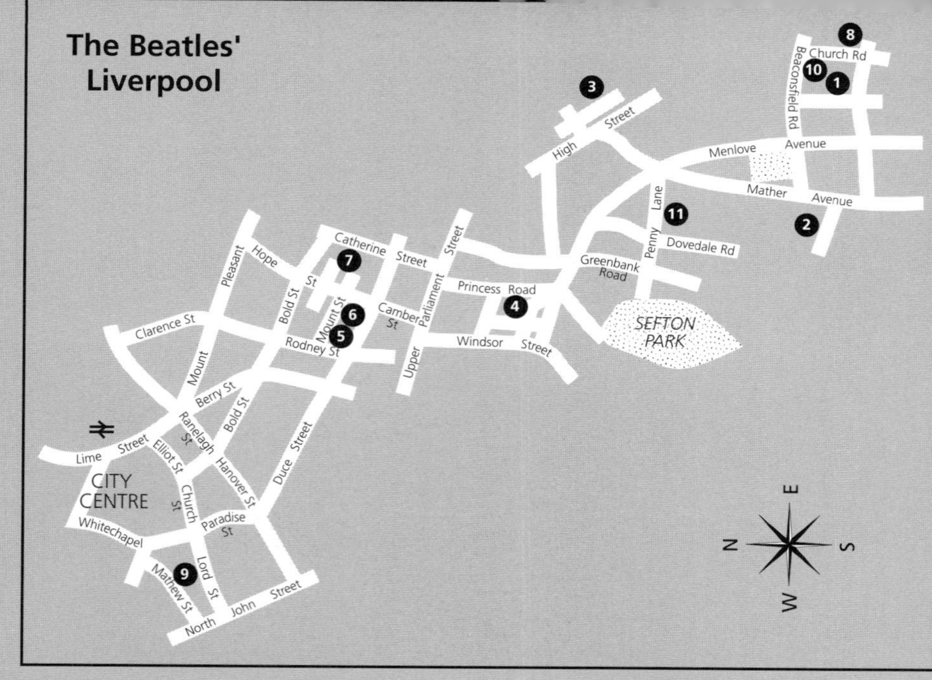
The Beatles' Liverpool
CITY CENTRE
Lime Street
Clarence St
Mount
Pleasant
Hope St
Bold St
Berry St
Ranelagh St
Elliot St
Church St
Whitechapel
Paradise St
Hanover St
Duce Street
Mathew St
Lord St
North John Street
Rodney St
Mount St
Catherine Street
Camber St
Upper Parliament Street
Princess Road
Windsor Street
High Street
Greenbank Road
Penny Lane
Dovedale Rd
SEFTON PARK
Menlove Avenue
Mather Avenue
Beaconsfield Rd
Church Rd
1
2
3
4
5
6
7
8
9
10
11
N
E
S
W

# Appendix The Beatles' Liverpool

ɅENDIPS CHILDHOOD HOME OF JOHN LENNON

**1** | Where: 251 Menlove Avenue, Woolton, 'Mendips'
Who: **JOHN LENNON**
When: 1945-1960

ennon was born at Oxford Street Maternity Hospital on 9 September 1940 and ved with his mother, Julia, at 9 Newcastle Road.

At the age of five, he moved to Mendips, home of his Aunt Mimi after the artime marriage of his parents had broken up.

He went to the primary school in Dovedale Road, before going to Quarry Bank rammar School, Harthill Road. He named his first band The Quarry Men, after e school.

**2** | Where: 20 Forthlin Road, Allerton
Who: **PAUL McCARTNEY**
When: Late 1940s-1963

ɔrn on 13 June 1942 at Walton Hospital, Rice Lane, McCartney first lived at 10 nbury Road, Anfield. His mother was a nurse and the family moved around ıtil settling in Allerton.

McCartney lived here until The Beatles moved to London in 1963. It was at this ›use that his mother died of breast cancer.

Before going to the Liverpool Institute, McCartney went to Joseph Williams imary School, Naylorsfield Road in Belle Valle.

McCartney still owns a house in Liverpool: 'Baskerville', on Rembrandt Avenue Heswall.

**3** | Where: 12 Arnold Grove, Wavertree
Who: **GEORGE HARRISON**
When: 24 February 1943

Harrison was born at his family's home and lived here for many years. They moved to 174 Mackets Lane, Hunts Cross in the late 1950s, where Harrison lived until he moved to London.

**THE EMPRESS PUB**
RINGO'S LOCAL

**4** | Where: 9 Madryn Street, Dingle
Who: **RINGO STARR**
When: 7 July 1940

Ringo Starr was born Richard Starkey at this house and lived here for the first fe years of his life. His mother swapped the house for 10 Admiral Grove, also in Dingle, in the mid-1940s. Starr lived there until 1964 when The Beatles moved t London.

He went to St Silas Primary School, Pengwern St and then to Dingle Vale Secondary Modern. He left school to play drums for several Liverpool bands, including Rory Storm and the Hurricanes.

The Empress Pub on High Park Street, Dingle featured on the cover of his 197 first solo album *Sentimental Journey*.

**5** | Where: Liverpool Institute, Mount Street
Who: **PAUL McCARTNEY & GEORGE HARRISON**
When: 1950s

McCartney and Harrison met at this grammar school. McCartney brought Harrison into The Beatles as a result of hearing him play at the school.

In the 1990s, Paul McCartney was behind the conversion of the building to tl Liverpool Institute for the Performing Arts.

**6** | Where: Liverpool Art College, Hope Street
Who: **JOHN LENNON & STUART SUTCLIFFE**
When: Early 1960s

At art college, Lennon met Cynthia Powell, his first wife, and Stuart Sutcliffe, the artist who was with The Beatles in their early months and died in Hamburg.

Lennon and Sutcliffe lived together at 3 Gambier Terrace whilst at college. In 1962, Lennon moved out when he married Cynthia at the registry office, 64 Mount Pleasant on 23 August, after discovering that she was pregnant. Paul McCartney was the best man and The Beatles played a gig later that night.

**7** | Where: 36 Falkner Street
Who: **BRIAN EPSTEIN**
When: Early 1960s

Brian Epstein, The Beatles' manager, allowed Lennon to use his flat, not far from the Art College, for a short honeymoon with Cynthia.

**8** | Where: St Peter's Church Hall, Church Road, Woolton
Who: **JOHN LENNON & PAUL McCARTNEY**
When: 6 July 1957

After a Quarry Men gig, the seventeen year old Lennon was introduced to McCartney. Impressing Lennon with his interest in skiffle, McCartney soon joined the band, making his first performance with them at the Conservative Club, Broad Lane, Norris Green.

**9** | Where: The Cavern, 10 Mathew St
When: March 1961-1963

The Beatles played here 292 times. This was where their future manager, Brian Epstein, came to see them after hearing their name at his record shop, NEMS at 12 Whitechapel.

The club was redeveloped in 1973.

**10** | Where: Salvation Army Children's home, Beaconsfield Road
When: 1960s

This children's home was better known as 'Strawberry Fields' to those who lived nearby. The young John Lennon would climb over the gates to play in the wooded grounds, close to Mendips, his Aunt Mimi's home.

**11** | Where: Penny Lane, Allerton
When: 1960s

The song *Penny Lane* describes this road. The barber shop, the roundabout and the fire station are all here, as described by Paul McCartney who wrote the song.

# Index